PHILOSOPHY *for* Busy People

Also by Alain Stephen

Why We Think the Things We Think

This Book Will Make You Think

PHILOSOPHY *for* Busy People

EVERYTHING YOU NEED TO KNOW

Alain Stephen

Michael O'Mara Books Limited

First published in Great Britain in 2019 by
Michael O'Mara Books Limited
9 Lion Yard
Tremadoc Road
London SW4 7NQ

A CIP catalogue record for this book is available from the British Library.

Papers used by Michael O'Mara Books Limited are natural, recyclable products made from wood grown in sustainable forests. The manufacturing processes conform to the environmental regulations of the country of origin.

ISBN: 978-1-78929-065-3 in hardback print format
ISBN: 978-1-78929-441-5 in paperback print format
ISBN: 978-1-78929-066-0 in ebook format

2 3 4 5 6 7 8 9 10

Designed and typeset by Design 23

Printed and bound by CPI Group (UK) Ltd, Croydon CR0 4YY

www.mombooks.com

CONTENTS

Truth is a thing of this world: it is produced only by virtue of multiple forms of constraint. And it induces regular effects of power. Each society has its regime of truth, its 'general politics' of truth: that is, the types of discourse which it accepts and makes function as true; the mechanisms and instances which enable one to distinguish true and false statements, the means by which each is sanctioned, the techniques and procedures accorded value in the acquisition of truth; the status of those who are charged with saying what counts as true.

MICHEL FOUCAULT (1977)

Introduction

THE SEARCH FOR TRUTH

In the modern age where the speed of life is bewildering at times, it is important to make space in our lives to think and reflect upon our assumptions and ideas. As Socrates (469–399 BC) is memorably alleged to have said in relation to the oracle: 'He, O men, is the wisest, who, like Socrates, knows that his wisdom is in truth worth nothing.' Or put another way, people who acknowledge that they don't actually know anything are wisest. This is not because they possess some higher wisdom than other mortals, but because they know that they do not. The search for truth and the asking of questions is the true purpose of philosophy.

For many an armchair philosopher, the title of this book probably sounds like a contradiction in terms. 'Philosophy' *and* 'busy'. Yet philosophy is by nature an active, 'considered' pursuit of knowledge. And what did the Ancients say?

- Aristotle (384–322 BC) promoted the idea of leisure; only the wise, Plato's 'philosopher Kings', were worthy of making decisions and promoting and cultivating virtuous living.

- Those 'Guardians', as Plato (*c.* 428–347 BC) termed them in *The Republic* (*c.* 380 BC), certainly weren't expected to work very hard, if actually work at all. It must have been lovely hanging out around the Lyceum (Aristotle's public place of learning established in 334 BC), comparing beard sizes and furrowing brows in quiet contemplation of what it all means.

So do busy people have time for philosophy in this day and age? How often do you hear people lament that 'there aren't enough hours in the day?'

> *'The unexamined life is not worth living.'*
>
> SOCRATES

The origins of the word 'philosophy', not surprisingly, derive from Ancient Greek. The root word '*philo*' means 'loving' or 'tending to/caring for', and '*sophos*' means 'wise' or 'wisdom'. So a philosopher is someone who loves and cares for wisdom and knowledge, while the standard dictionary definition of 'philosophy' is 'the study of the fundamental nature of knowledge, reality and existence', i.e. trying to discover what it all means: who are we and why are we here?

A worthy aim, but where to start? There are thousands of years of human thought to wade through; diverse and contradictory ideas and concepts, all devoted towards establishing fundamental truths about our existence as sentient beings. But if, as I am suggesting, philosophy is about unearthing truth, where can we find it and how to begin our search?

This book is your 'philosophy primer' – an easily digestible exploration that's structured thematically – of the key concepts and areas of knowledge that are integral to human life and thought. Think of it as a tasting menu, serving up little plates of tasty morsels of philosophy.

The Philosophy of Happiness (see Chapter 1) is a good first topic. Plato held that happiness was the ultimate goal of existence, hence his concept of *Eudaimonia,* which he describes in the Ancient Greek dictionary *Definitions* as 'The good composed of all goods; an ability which suffices for living well; perfection in respect of virtue; resources sufficient for a living creature.' But Plato's contemporary, Aristotle, points out that while saying the desire to live well is surely self-evident – nobody in their right mind would wish to live badly or lead an unhappy life – the real question is specifying what areas and activities enable one to live well and achieve happiness. So the Philosophy of Happiness means going back to Ancient Greece, then to China and India before jumping forward several thousand years to Denmark, 'the happiest country' in the world. It is not surprising that the same things that troubled and perplexed the Ancients are still major concerns in our search for wellbeing. And one of the key issues in the pursuit of *Eudaimonia* is the extent to which our personal pursuit of happiness impacts on and affects the people around us, and our wider communities, and the world in general.

Chapter 2, The Philosophy of Ethics and Morality, delves into the notions of 'right' and 'wrong' – the true and the false. The word 'truth' is derived from the Old English '*trīewþ*' which had two meanings, in its various inflections: either the quality of honesty, faithfulness and loyalty (thus 'being true to oneself'), or something – an object or concept, physical or metaphysical – that is constant and unchanging. St Thomas Aquinas (1225–74) goes further and states that truth is 'the conformity of the mind to the objects', *ergo* if we trust and process the information we receive through our sensory perceptions and neither deny nor distort them in our minds, we arrive at what is known as 'the correspondence theory of truth'. Put crudely, if you pick up a hammer and bash somebody over the head, the result is self-apparent.

The Philosophy of Science (Chapter 3) is a key issue, with truth corresponding to our perception of objects and ideas. History is littered with examples of what people believed to be scientifically true, subsequently being proved false. So how do we respond to St Thomas's 'theory of truth' when what is true in one epoch might not be so in the next? How do we determine concrete facts about the universe and everything therein? And, increasingly, commentators have flagged up the blurring of truth with opinion – facts deployed in support of opinion and, vice versa, opinion presented as facts.

Chapter 4 and The Philosophy of Politics and Power looks at the structures and mechanisms of how social organization strives to achieve *Eudaimonia* in the Aristotelian sense, or at least present the illusion of it. The French philosopher and historian Michel Foucault (1926–84) states: 'Each society has its regime of truth.' He goes on to suggest that the true duty of philosophers is to unmask 'the mechanisms and instances which enable one to distinguish true and false statements'. This has become progressively difficult in the current political and social climate, as it appears increasingly that we are in an age where the search for a cogent expression of truth, in the historical and authentic sense, has become one of finding plausible ways *not* to present the truth but instead to mask and blur how information is presented (but that is only an opinion, not a 'fact'). Power, for Foucault, 'is everywhere' – concealed in institutions and discourses.

The Philosophy of Religion (Chapter 5) is fascinating in both a historical and contemporary sense as it feeds into current debates on the teaching of creationism or 'intelligent design' in US schools. It is apposite also to look back at just how truthful virtues of 'honesty, faithfulness and loyalty' are being promoted.

Chapter 6 and The Philosophy of Language tackles how words are used. How is meaning transmitted, received and distorted? It has been said that we are living in an era of 'post-truth', which the African-born philosopher A.C. Grayling (b. 1949) defines as a cultural phenomenon where 'opinion is worth more than the facts'. Judgements are made on the basis of feelings and emotions as opposed to concrete, irrefutable facts. The search for truth goes on. Which brings us to …

The final two chapters cover The Philosophy of Love, which I'd hoped might wrap up the whistle-stop charge through the history of thought on a positive note.

However, the gloomy musings of Jean-Paul Sartre (1905–80) and Friedrich Nietzsche (1844–1900) scuppered that plan, and we end with The Philosophy of the Future, a generalized discussion on contemporary thought while speculating what the future of philosophy may look like.

How to handle Hegel?

The work of Georg Wilhelm Hegel (1770–1831) may raise a few eyebrows. His pursuit of absolute realism and dialectical method is notoriously complex as it concerns itself with oppositions and contradictions (thesis and anti-thesis) in the search for synthesis or higher truth. Hegel is hard to grasp – i.e. really hard – and not someone to read for pleasure. One common criticism of his work is that he often assumes readers have a thorough grounding in the history of philosophical thought, and his style is certainly not very clear or concise, being unsuitable for busy people. Although his influence on analytic philosophy is without question, a casual reader will find more food for thought and have much more fun reading Paul Feyerabend's *Against Method* or Nietzsche's entertaining aphorisms in *Human, All Too Human*. Try Hegel if you want, but be warned ...

1

What you need to know about THE PHILOSOPHY OF HAPPINESS

Philosophers have been contemplating questions of happiness since the fifth century BC, i.e. what constitutes happiness? and how do we achieve it? Furthermore, how do we know when we are truly happy? The concept of happiness is integral to the meaning of life and the antidote to conflict and strife, and yet it remains elusive and abstract.

SOCRATES AND PLATO – THE BEDROCK OF WESTERN PHILOSOPHY

Considered the godfather of western philosophy, Socrates (469–399 BC) lived in Athens his entire life, challenging his fellow Athenians with questions concerning truth and justice. He followed two key maxims, first that 'the unexamined life is not worth living' and second that the bedrock of his wisdom was the understanding that he actually knew 'nothing' at all. However, the concept of happiness was central to Socrates' thoughts and ideas, and centred on the notion that happiness is obtainable by gaining ownership of one's desires to establish harmony in the human soul. This process, he maintained, would eventually produce a divine state of inner tranquillity, free from the corrupting forces of the external world. Although Socrates wrote down none of his ideas, his profound influence on his disciple Plato and his subsequent pupil Aristotle have had an immeasurable influence on the development of western philosophy.

Plato's Academy

Plato set up his school for philosophers in a grove dedicated to the hero Akademus, which explains why it came to be known as the Academy, which in turn explains why scholarly types are known as academics.

The prevailing view of happiness in Socrates' time was firmly embedded in metaphysical notions of fate and the will of the gods. Socrates suggested that happiness wasn't actually a matter of chance, but could be obtained through human endeavour and careful contemplation of the forces effecting human life. Happiness was viewed as a blessing bestowed upon people whom the gods favoured, and to seek it represented hubris and conceit that would only result in your downfall. This view is commonly dramatized in classical Greek tragedies where the central protagonists are the unwitting architects of their own fate.

Socrates also argued that the key to happiness meant shifting the emphasis away from the pleasures of the body and material concerns of the world to focus on the soul. By harmonizing our desires, he argued, we can learn to pacify the mind and achieve a divine-like state of tranquillity.

Plato (428–347 BC) presented Socrates' views in a series of works known as *The Dialogues*. These works are:

- Socrates' conversations with a range of different people: politicians, playwrights, prominent members of Athenian society, students and friends.

- Each dialogue consists of Socrates challenging these people to explain the basis of their beliefs.

- Through an extended process of question and answer – i.e. the Socratic method – Socrates unpicks their arguments and propositions to expose the false logic in their reasoning, and highlight flaws and contradictions.

- The dialogue known as *The Symposium* is an apposite example of both the Socratic method and Socrates' ideas on happiness.

The Symposium takes place at a dinner party, and the subject of happiness arises as each of the guests is invited to make a speech in honour of Eros, the god of love and desire. Eryximachus, a prominent Athenian physician, argues that Eros is the god most capable of bestowing happiness, and the playwright Aristophanes agrees, claiming that Eros is 'that helper of mankind… who eliminates those evils whose cure brings the greatest happiness to the human race'. Eryximachus' position is that Eros, as the god of love, provides the force that gives life to all things, including human desire, and therefore is the source of goodness in the world. Aristophanes expands this point by arguing that Eros is the potency that reunites humans through love, and explicitly through sex. But Socrates has a problem with Eros.

He suggests that Eros has a darker side, since, as the

representation of desire, he is constantly in a state of longing that can never be satisfied or sated. In this sense Eros cannot be considered a true god because divinity, by definition, must be eternal and self-sufficient. But Socrates then switches emphasis and argues that Eros is vitally important in the human quest for happiness as he represents the transition between the human and the divine. Eros provides the impetus behind desire, which starts by seeking physical pleasures but can be restrained and channelled in the pursuit of the higher aspects of the mind.

Socrates' argument is that the love of beautiful things is transient and shallow, but simultaneously that the concept of beauty is the key to happiness and fulfilment. And contemplating beauty in and of itself means that the soul will be in harmony. Socrates believes this process to be a moment of rapture or epiphany since the truth of one's existence is realized:

> *If man's life is ever worth the living, it is when he has attained this vision of the soul of beauty. And once you have seen it you will never be seduced again by the charm of gold, of dress … you will care nothing for the beauties that used to take your breath away … and when one discerns this beauty one will perceive the true virtue, not virtue's semblance.*
>
> SOCRATES

Socrates' constant questioning of received wisdom and widely held beliefs eventually put him at loggerheads with the Athenian authorities, and he was accused and put on trial for 'corrupting the young' and 'denying the gods'. Socrates was found guilty, albeit by a kangaroo court, and given the option of living in exile or the death penalty. True to his convictions, he chose death because he believed that to live in exile would violate his principles of freedom of thought. He died by drinking a potion of hemlock and is said to have been cheerfully expounding his philosophy right to the end.

'HAPPINESS IS THE PATH'

Siddhārtha Gautama was a spiritual leader and philosopher from the eastern part of ancient India (modern day Nepal) who lived around 500 BC. The teachings of Siddhārtha form the bedrock of Buddhism and follow what is known as 'the middle path' to enlightenment, which seeks a harmonious balance between the pleasures of the senses and asceticism.

The Buddha's wisdom was originally passed down orally by his followers after his death and didn't appear in written form until several hundred years later. For Siddhārtha, happiness is not an end in itself but a matter of process: 'There is no path to happiness: happiness is

Jon Kabat-Zinn and mindfulness

The practice of reflective meditation in the philosophy of Siddhārtha Gautama and Buddhist teachings has had a significant impact on modern approaches to psychotherapy, such as Cognitive Behavioural Therapy (CBT) and mindfulness.

The American academic Jon Kabat-Zinn developed his interest in Buddhism in the late 1970s and researched ways in which meditative practices could be used in medicine. He set up the Stress Reduction Clinic at the University of Massachusetts Medical School and developed an eight-week programme of meditation and Hatha yoga – called Mindfulness Based Stress Reduction (MBSR) – to combat stress and anxiety. MBSR proved a great success and Kabat-Zinn subsequently developed mindfulness as a therapeutic tool to combat other medical conditions, including depression, psychosis and persistent pain.

the path.' In other words, take pleasure and fulfilment in the journey, the moment, and not in striving to reach an idealized destination.

This view suggests that happiness is impermanent and transient, incapable of providing lasting contentment and therefore actually leads to pain and the Buddhist concept of *saṃsāra* – an endless cycle of rebirth, suffering and death. In order to escape *saṃsāra* and reach *nirvana* – a state of spiritual completeness – the Buddha preaches avoiding damaging desires through reflective meditation, which achieves 'liberating insight'. The key is to find ways to enjoy the journey, the present lived experience, and eschew destructive restlessness about the future or the past.

Mindfulness

The guiding principles of mindfulness are to create room in our lives to make clearer choices, garner more control through calm reflection, make positive decisions and ultimately find happiness by noticing the positive details of our lives and relationships. Although Jon Kabat-Zinn (see box, above) has played down the influence that Buddhist philosophy had on his therapies, preferring to state that mindfulness is set within a scientific and medical framework and not a religious belief system, there are clear echoes of Siddhārtha Gautama's mantra that 'happiness is the path'.

MEANWHILE, IN CHINA, WHAT *DID* CONFUCIUS SAY?

Similar ideas on the philosophy of happiness and the power of positive thinking can be found in the teachings of Confucius (551 BC–479 BC), who lived in the same era as Siddhārtha Gautama. Confucius is known for his very quotable aphorisms, and some academics argue that they are the basis of a secular moral code known as Confucianism, and not a form of religion. The *Analects*, a collection of conversations between Confucius and his disciples that was compiled by his followers after his death, are at the centre of Confucianism. When asked to define the nature of happiness, Confucius replied: 'The more man meditates upon good thoughts, the better will be his world and the world at large.'

This mantra was expanded by his contemporary Lao Tzu (also known as 'Laozi' or 'the old master') in his classic philosophical text *Tao Te Ching*. Regarded as the founder of the ancient Chinese philosophy of Taoism, Lao Tzu is a semi-mythical figure. There's little historical evidence about him, just colourful folk tales about him visiting western lands on the back of a water buffalo and various contradictory legends. But we can say:

- Modern scholars of ancient Chinese culture have reached a general consensus that *Tao Te Ching* was written and compiled by several different people on account of the unevenness of the rhetorical methods. Classical Confucius-style aphorisms are mixed in with contrasting oppositions, presumably to highlight the fallacy of implacable wisdom.

- An essential ingredient of Taoism is the concept of *wu wei*, which translates ambiguously as 'non-action' or 'acting through inaction'.

- The Tao is the natural state of life, allegorically a flowing river or stream. But ideologies, ambitions and desires create conflict with the Tao and hinder the natural flow of the river.

- However, by embodying virtues of humility and simplicity and the meditative practice of *zuowang* (entering a trance-like state where the mind is emptied of all thoughts of selfhood and identity, i.e. 'sitting in oblivion'), the eternal river will flow around these self-imposed obstructions to the Tao.

- In *Tao Te Ching*, Lao Tzu states: 'If you are depressed you are living in the past, if you are anxious you are living in the future, if you are at peace you are living in the present.'

DEMOCRITUS: 'THE LAUGHING PHILOSOPHER'

Democritus (460–370 BC), whose Greek name means 'chosen by the people', was born in the ancient Greek city of Abdera, in the region of Thrace, a thriving port close to the border with modern Turkey. Although known principally as one of the co-founders of the Atomist school of thought, he is thought to have written over sixty works on a variety of subjects including morality, ethics, and how to live a happy life. Contemporary accounts of Democritus' life portray him as an ebullient and jaunty personality, which is why he was called 'the laughing philosopher'. Alongside his scientific and philosophical investigations and writings, he is reported to have travelled widely, visiting the ancient city of Babylon and trekking around Egypt, North Africa and India.

Democritus' contribution to the philosophy of happiness consists of a series of quotes and aphorisms that survive in fragments attributed to him by other writers and philosophers, rather than to any school of thought or work. In keeping with his good-natured disposition, he valued cheerfulness as a means of maintaining the purity of the soul: 'Happiness does not dwell in flocks of cattle or in pots of gold. Happiness, like unhappiness, is a property of the soul.'

Democritus preached that human life is brittle, short and riddled with anxieties and problems. Also, the majority of difficulties that lead to unhappiness stem from yearning for what we don't have (e.g. money, status and power) instead of valuing what we do have, and measuring hardship by what we really need in order to be happy. He argued: 'Cheerfulness or wellbeing is created in people through a harmonious life of moderation of enjoyment. Excess and want are forever changing and cause great disturbance in the soul, and souls that are stirred by great disturbances are neither stable nor cheerful.'

In short, Democritus believed in a life of contented moderation and being wary of things that are 'envied or admired' by other people. By careful observation of 'lives in distress and suffering' one will realize that one's own life of contented moderation is of infinitely greater value and, by resisting a desire for more, one 'will cease to suffer in the soul, live more serenely and expel the curses of life – envy, jealousy and spite'.

The death of Democritus and the power of freshly baked bread

Thesmophoria was one of the most important female-only religious festivals in the Ancient Greek calendar. It was held in honour of the goddess Demeter and her daughter Persephone, and men were banned. The offering of worship, sacrifices and tributes to the goddesses was intended to promote female and agricultural fertility, providing children and bountiful crops. One tradition involved women baking bread in the shape of giant phalluses and placing them upon an altar.

Democritus' sister had been chosen to be a 'bailer' at the festival – women who worshipped before the altars in a trance-like state of ritual purity – and was distressed that she would have to leave the then ailing Democritus to die alone. He assured her he would still be alive when she returned and, true to his word and to her astonishment, he was still hanging on at the end of the festivities. He claimed that he'd managed to hold out by inhaling the smell of freshly baked bread, which permeated the air during Thesmophoria.

THE AESTHETIC VERSUS THE ETHICAL LIFE

The three aspects of the philosophy of happiness that keep recurring are: a concentration on rejecting the damaging influence of desire; learning to respect our lives as they are lived; and valuing moderation.

The Danish-born philosopher Søren Kierkegaard (1813–55) also embraced the virtues of living in the moment when he wrote his 1844 treatise on ethics, *Either, Or*. Often considered a precursor to existentialism, which is sometimes erroneously portrayed as a wilfully gloomy philosophy, Kierkegaard drew a distinction between the aesthetic and the truly ethical life. The aesthetic is characterized by gratification of desire and ambition, and leads to anxiety and conflict of free will. He believed that once people reject the aesthetic life, they are free to experience life as it is and derive happiness and satisfaction from their experiences: 'Life is not a problem to be solved but a reality to be experienced.'

The questions posed by the philosophy of happiness are in essence something of a paradox. Throughout two millennia, philosophers attempting to define happiness and how to attain it have actually focused on the factors that hinder our capacity to be happy, and the causes of misery and despair. From Socrates to Kierkegaard, thinkers have rejected desire, blind ambition and sensory pleasure as routes to happiness, in favour of merely relishing the moment and enjoying the here and now. As the stoic Roman philosopher Seneca (4 BC–AD 65) wrote in his collection of moral essays: 'The greatest blessings of mankind are within us and within our reach. A wise man is content with his lot, whatever it may be, without wishing for what he has not.'

The origins of angst

Kierkegaard introduced the now widely used word 'angst' – in Danish it means 'anxiety' or 'dread', and we use it to describe the sense of profound insecurity and fear. He first used it in his book *The Concept of Anxiety* (1844), arguing that freedom of choice leaves people in a perpetual state of anxiety about their responsibilities to God. For later existentialists it was more a case of responsibilities to oneself, one's principles and other people.

Why is Denmark the happiest country in the world?

In March 2018, the World Happiness Report – an annual survey of 155 countries – ranked Denmark as the world's happiest country for the seventh consecutive year. Studies of 'subjective well-being' are conducted through scientific analysis of objective data on crime figures, average income, civic engagements and health. This data is then contrasted with qualitative analysis of surveys on positive and negative emotions, and general personal reflections. Although Denmark has political stability, high quality, free-of-charge health care and education systems, and relatively low crime rates, the cost of living is high, as are taxes.

Where Denmark comes out on top, though, is in the more subjective indicators of happiness, most notably in a Danish cultural phenomenon known as '*hygge*'.

Hygge roughly translates as 'cosy' or 'intimate', and is used in relation to shared experiences with others and harmonious social interactions. It can be applied to an enjoyable lunch with an old friend, a family picnic by the seaside or a warming cup of hot chocolate by a roaring fire on a cold winter's night. The essence of *hygge* is that it relates to balanced, simple contact with other people and enjoying the moment with them. The word is used in multiple contexts; it is, for example, customary to thank

Kim Kierkegaardashian: the sage of Twitter

In 2012, a Twitter account appeared under the name of Kim Kierkegaardashian and quickly established a cult following. Combining the philosophy of the Danish existentialist philosopher Søren Kierkegaard with the fashion and beauty tips, and general celebrity musings of reality TV star Kim Kardashian, Kim's clever Twitter mash-ups include: 'Just got the best spray tan!!! There is an indescribable joy which glows through us unaccountably' and 'I scarcely recognize myself, my mind is like a turbulent sea, I am testing new mascara.'

Inevitably, the success of Ms Kim Kierkegaardashian has led to copycat accounts with characters such as Kantye West humorously fusing the eighteenth-century enlightenment philosophy of Immanuel Kant with the Twitter rantings of rapper Kanye West.

the hosts of a dinner party by declaring the evening '*hyggelige*', in fact it would be ill-mannered not to.

Hygge has become so engrained in the Danish psyche and culture that psychological studies have been undertaken to determine how other countries can foster mutual appreciation of simple, shared pleasures and experiences. Kierkegaard, although he didn't coin the phrase, wrote extensively on living as an experience that frees us of anxiety, stress and despair and so was, in a sense, an early proponent of *hygge*.

2

What you need to know about

THE PHILOSOPHY OF ETHICS AND MORALITY

These two branches of philosophy – ethics and morality – are often indistinguishable. On a basic level a difference does exist, but philosophers have struggled to untangle one from the other.

THE GREAT DIVIDE

The word 'ethics' derives from the Ancient Greek '*ēthikós*', meaning 'relating to one's character', and the word 'morals' derives from the Latin '*mos*' (by extension '*moralis*') meaning 'customs'.

The irony is that the word '*moralis*' is thought to have first been coined by the Roman philosopher and historian

Cicero (106 BC–43 BC) in an attempt to translate the Greek concept of *ēthikós* into Latin. Now, the broad distinction is that ethics relates to fundamental questions relating to human character and defining how we, as individuals, should live our lives, particularly when faced with difficult decisions. Morals, however, relate to customs or practices derived from a set of guidelines; for example, Christian morality is predominately derived from the teachings of the Bible.

There are problems, nevertheless, with making clear distinctions between ethics and morals. Many modern institutions, from medicine to the law, from business to the mass media, have supposedly transparent ethical codes. And it's assumed they are drawn up via a consensus of the right way to act under certain circumstances and in particular situations. Current debates on euthanasia in the medical profession provide a useful example of how separating ethics from morals or morality can be confusing and problematic, for while it is possible to argue that assisted suicide contravenes the Hippocratic Oath, conversely you can question the morality of allowing a patient to suffer unnecessarily. So, for reasons of clarity, I'll look at ethics as a branch of philosophy that deals with questions of human morality by defining concepts such as good and evil, right and wrong, virtue and vice, and justice and crime.

Within the philosophy of ethics there are three widely recognized schools or lines of inquiry. They are:

- *Normative ethics* – the most traditional school, dating back to Ancient Greece, which tackles the practical questions, how to determine the 'right' course of action or how to live a 'just or righteous life'.

- *Meta-ethics* – which approaches the theoretical meaning and reference of moral propositions, and how it is possible (or impossible) to determine their truth value.

- *Applied ethics* – involving questions of obligation in relation to our actions, either individually or collectively.

NORMATIVE ETHICS: HOW TO LIVE?

Sometimes called prescriptive ethics, normative ethics are primarily concerned with establishing how things should or ought to be. They attempt to value what makes particular actions right or wrong, or good or bad. The goal, in principle, is to come to an understanding of a set of overarching principles or guidelines to govern actions in a morally correct way. Within the broad study of normative ethics are three differing, yet inter-related, approaches: *consequentialism*, *deontology* and *virtue ethics*.

Consequentialism: do the ends justify the means?

Consequentialism is often referred to in philosophical circles as a teleological model for ethics. The Greek word '*telos*' means 'goal' or 'purpose' and '*logos*' 'reason' or 'meaning'. So consequentialism, or teleological, ethics argue that the moral value of a certain action is dependent on the action's consequence or result. This view holds that a morally right or correct action in a given situation is one that produces a good outcome, and that a morally wrong action produces or has implicitly bad consequences. And within this paradigm, consequentialist theories confront questions such as:

- What form of consequences amount to being good consequences?
- Who, or what, principally benefits from a particular moral action?
- How do we judge the value of consequences, and who decides if they are good or bad?

The ancient Greek philosopher Epicurus (341 BC–270 BC) is often called the forefather of consequentialist ethics. He came from the hedonist school of Greek philosophy, which believed that pleasure was the greatest good in human life, the ultimate goal of existence. Hedonism, however, is frequently misinterpreted, particularly today, as being the unabashed pursuit of the pleasures of the senses. Not so – the ancient hedonists defined pleasure primarily as living without pain and achieving a state of blissful tranquillity. This state of *nirvana* could be achieved by developing *ataraxia* (freedom from fear), freedom from anguish (mental pain) and *aponia* (freedom from bodily pain).

In terms of consequentialist ethics, pursuing a course of action that gives the most pleasure was seen as the right consequence. However, and it is at this point that the teachings of Epicurus and other hedonists have been misunderstood, if the desire for pleasure ultimately brings pain then the consequence was a bad choice. For example, Epicurus preached moderation and taking pleasure in the simple things in life, such as food and shelter, and not being driven by wealth and material objects. A glass of wine with dinner should be enjoyed, but greedily drinking a whole carafe will likely cause discomfort, disorientation and possibly sickness. So moderation in this example equals wisdom, and an ability to control desires for the greater good of happiness and serenity.

By the nineteenth century, consequentialist ethics had shifted from a concentration on individual 'happiness' to 'collective happiness' via the formulation of utilitarianism (see Chapter 4) and the work of Jeremy Bentham (1748–1832) and John Stuart Mill (1806–73). But what does it involve?

- The principal focus of utilitarianism is taking the word utility to define general welfare or happiness, and Mill's interpretation was that, in this sense, 'utility' is the consequence of good actions.

- Utility is only measurable in terms of people performing actions for the pursuit of social utility or the wellbeing of many people, not just individuals.

- In his work *Utilitarianism* (1863), Mill argues that people, in essence, really do desire happiness – why would anyone wish to be unhappy? Since each individual desires their own happiness, it must follow that we all desire the happiness of everyone, and by doing so contribute to a larger social utility.

- So, an action that has, as a consequence, the greatest pleasure for the utility of society is the best possible course of action.

- Mill's view echoed that of his mentor and one-time teacher Bentham in his famous axiom: 'The greatest happiness of the greatest number is the foundation of morals.'

Act Utilitarianism versus Rule Utilitarianism

Within utilitarianism there are two distinct forms known as Act Utilitarianism and Rule Utilitarianism. In Act Utilitarianism the principle of utility or the consequence that brings about the most happiness is evaluated according to an either/or choice in a given situation. In Rule Utilitarianism the principle of utility determines the validity of the accepted rules of correct conduct or a set of moral principles or rules. Confused? Here's an example.

A relative has a heart attack – an ambulance is called but being 6 am on a public holiday the emergency services are short-staffed; time is crucial so you drive them to hospital. When the traffic lights turn red, do you jump them and increase the chances of saving a life or wait for the lights to turn green?

Act Utilitarian answer: jump the red light. Although breaking the law, this gives a better chance of utility as it increases the chances of saving a life. Given the timing there is very little traffic on the road and the chances of causing an accident are minimal and, although you may get photographed by a traffic camera and taken to court, it is a chance you are willing to take for the greater good.

Rule Utilitarian answer: wait for the light to change. The reckless consequence of jumping the red light could cause an accident resulting in injury and possible loss of life. The rule to stop at a red light is to help protect all road-users and to safeguard against irresponsible driving. If everyone jumped a red light every time they were in a hurry there would be carnage and the 'utility' value of the rule would be redundant.

Act Utilitarians would argue that the selfless act of doing everything in one's power to try and save a life remained the right option, regardless of a possibly catastrophic outcome. Should the driver get to the hospital unscathed, then 'the ends justify the means'. *Rule Utilitarians* believe that the determination of right or wrong in this situation is dependent on the rationale behind the rule, regardless of any mitigating circumstances.

Deontology: a moral obligation

Deontology is the theory of ethics that centres on the apparent and intrinsic 'right' or 'wrong' of an act, as opposed to the consequences of that act. In some senses, Rule Utilitarianism (see above) can be read as a form of deontology as it proposes that certain rules and duties are always ethically correct. Derived from the Ancient Greek word '*deon*', meaning 'duty', deontology contends that decisions on how to act and particular situations are dependent upon a consideration of one's duty to oneself, and to the rights and wellbeing of others – what we'd call a 'moral obligation'. There are, however, different categories of deontological ethics as moral obligations may arise from an external or internal source, such as a set of rules inherent to the universe (the Ancient Greek model known as ethical naturalism), religious law, or a set of personal or cultural values. But regardless of the nature of the source of the obligation, internal or external, conflict can occur with personal desires.

Divine command theory: God told me to do it

Traditional forms of deontological ethics are centred around religion and the concept of the Divine Command theory, a form of deontology that states that an action is right if God has decreed that it is right, and that an act is obligatory if and only if – and because – it is commanded by God. Thus, moral obligations arise from God's commands, and the 'rightness' of any action depends on that action being performed because it is a duty.

Organized religions, for better or worse, have utilized Divine Command theory as a means of acquiring power and control over societies and groups. The notion that an act is right regardless of the consequences because, at base level, it is God's will is clearly problematic. Nonetheless, this form of deontological ethics has survived since the early Middle Ages, being pervasive in different religions across the world and manifesting itself in a variety of forms – from simple customs to terrorist atrocities. This is not to say that the theory is necessarily a negative or restricting concept; on the contrary, many so-called 'commands' are positive and altruistic.

Modern theology and religious doctrine is far more sympathetic to individual choice than in the days of René Descartes (1596–1650) and yet, despite the constraints of his time, Descartes made a clear distinction between reason and the concept of personal virtue. Our capacity for reason was, for Descartes, at the centre of human knowledge, bequeathed to humans by 'the perfect being'. God provided us with the capacity to think (*cogito ergo sum* – I think therefore I am), and to reason is sufficient in the search for the good and righteous that we should seek. This leads to developing virtues that are found in the correct reasoning that guides our actions in any situation, and leads us towards fulfilment and happiness.

So, the cultivation of reason is the key to a balanced attitude to living. As Descartes states in his work *Principles of Philosophy* (1647): 'True philosophy … teaches that even amidst the saddest disasters and most bitter pains we can always be content, provided that we know how to use our reason.' He defined philosophy as 'the study of wisdom, and by "wisdom" is meant not only prudence in our everyday affairs but also a perfect knowledge of all things that mankind is capable of knowing, both for the conduct of life and for the preservation of health and the discovery of all manner of skills.' Although Descartes does not explicitly evoke the Divine Command theory, he argues that as he has an idea of God in his mind, God must exist. In his *Meditations* (1641), Descartes states 'that the mere fact that I exist and have within me an idea of a most perfect being, that is, God, provides a very clear proof that God indeed exists ... it is no surprise that God, in creating me, should have placed this idea in me to be, as it were, the mark of the craftsman stamped on his work'. Therefore, whatever Descartes, through the application of reason and the development of wisdom, concludes to be morally true is also that which God decrees to be morally true or right.

Immanuel Kant and the categorical imperative

Immanuel Kant (1724–1804) was a leading figure in the German Enlightenment and, following on from Descartes, his philosophy is rooted very much in the human capacity for reason. Where Kant differs from Descartes, however, is in taking a secular approach to deontology as opposed to the (albeit somewhat vague in the case of his predecessor) religious approach. Kant also rejected consequentialism as a basis for moral judgements or actions as he believed in a form of universal duty derived from the application of reason. For Kant, some actions are always wrong, regardless of the outcome, and it is the motives of the person who carries out the action that determines if they are right or wrong and not the consequences of the action.

Kant, the human clock

According to the German-Jewish poet, essayist and literary critic, Heinrich Heine (1797–1856) in his book *On the History of Religion and Philosophy in Germany* (1832), Kant was a man of great precision, particularly in his timekeeping. 'I do not believe that the great clock of the cathedral [in Konigsberg] performed in a more passionless and methodical manner in its daily routine than did its townsman, Immanuel Kant. Rising in the morning, coffee drinking, writing, reading lectures, dining, walking, everything had its appointed time, and the neighbours knew it was exactly half-past three when Immanuel Kant stepped forth from his house in his grey, tight-fitting coat, with his Spanish cane in hand, and betook himself to the little linden avenue, called to this day [the] "Philosopher's Walk".'

In his pioneering treatise *Groundwork of the Metaphysics of Morals* (1785), Kant outlines three formulations that contribute to what he termed the categorical imperative, a moral framework that represents the duty of human will when freed from external influences and forces. In the first formulation, Kant draws a distinction between what he calls 'perfect duties' and 'imperfect duties'. The former consists of universal maxims that can be applied to everyone and are not contingent on circumstances. The latter are more fluid situations, open to different interpretations, and are dependent upon context and circumstance.

Kant uses the word maxim to mean the motivating principle behind the action and states in the first formulation, that people should 'Act only according to that maxim whereby you can at the same time will that it should become a universal law without contradiction.' Put simply, and free from Kant's often impenetrable terminology, the first formulation can be summarized along the lines of the 'golden rule' or 'ethic of reciprocity' which states 'do unto others as one would have done unto oneself'.

Kant's 'imperfect duties' concern the treatment of others and argue that people should 'act in such a way that you treat humanity, whether in your own person or in the person of any other, never merely as a means to an end but always at the same time as an end'. Kant believed that to use other people in actions as a means to an end, regardless of outcome, was morally wrong as this denied that person their own free will and rights.

Kant's third and final formulation concerns the application of moral duties to communities and states that 'every rational being must so act as if he were through his maxim always a legislating member in the universal kingdom of ends'. In some ways this has echoes of utilitarianism's insistence on the validity of an action being determined by the amount of good imparted to the greatest number. Kant is stating that expressions of human will should be considered moral (i.e. perfect) duties provided everyone abides by them as universal laws. If, for example, it is wrong to lie, then this must be universally adopted by all as a maxim because lying disrupts trust and notions of truth.

One of the problems with Kant's deontology is that because it eschews any consideration of outcomes in its assessment of right or wrong, it lacks flexibility when faced with problematical contexts. There are situations when lying could trump the universal law as it may avoid a catastrophe. The classic test of this universal law is known as Kant's Axe Murderer Dilemma, which asks if it's 'right to tell a lie if it may save a life?' and, in this respect, it appears to fail along similar lines to the opposition between Rule Utilitarianism and Act Utilitarianism (see page 39).

Man, being condemned to be free, carries the weight of the whole world on his shoulders; he is responsible for the world and for himself as a way of being.

JEAN-PAUL SARTRE *BEING AND NOTHINGNESS*

Virtue ethics: how to be a virtuous person

Virtue ethics is a normative ethical theory which differs from deontology and consequentialism in that the focus shifts from evaluating actions (and consequences) and the moral value thereof, to emphasizing virtues of mind and character. Virtue ethics discusses the nature and definition of virtues: which aspects of individual character can be deemed virtuous? How are they acquired and applied? Are individual virtues part of universal human nature or do they derive from cultural plurality?

Aristotle in the *Nicomachean Ethics* outlined eighteen 'virtues' required to live a virtuous life, making a distinction between virtues pertaining to emotions and desires (moral virtues) and virtues of the mind (intellectual virtues).

Moral Virtues

- *Courage* – in facing individual fears
- *Temperance* – in matters of pleasure and pain
- *Liberality* – generosity with wealth and possessions
- *Magnificence* – taken to mean prudence when exhibiting wealth and possessions

- *Magnanimity* – humbleness when honour is bestowed upon an individual
- *Proper ambition* – realistic desire for power and influence
- *Truthfulness* – in self-expression
- *Wittiness* – cheerfulness in conversation
- *Friendliness* – in social conduct
- *Modesty* – in the face of shame or shamelessness
- *Righteous indignation* – in the face of injury or hurt to ourselves or others

Intellectual virtues

- *Intelligence* – in understanding what is true and real
- *Science* – in understanding the natural world
- *Theoretical wisdom* – in understanding fundamental truths and applying reason
- *Understanding* – comprehending the ideas and thoughts of others
- *Practical wisdom* – in applying actions to changing circumstances
- *Common sense* – sympathy and understanding in passing judgement
- *Technique* – skill in art or craftsmanship

As virtue ethics focuses on how a person is as opposed to what they do, it attempts to identify the characteristics that make a moral or virtuous individual. In this respect the actions of a person are merely a manifestation of their virtuous inner self – their personal morality. Actions (or consequences) in themselves cannot be deemed as adequate reflections of morality as this limits virtue to practical deeds and situations rather than an all-encompassing code to live by. Virtue ethics, therefore, strives for a morality where an individual would make consistently moral choices in all situations.

One of the principle objections to virtue ethics is disagreement over what constitutes a 'virtue' and if this can be adequately applied across different cultures and circumstances. Or, put another way, is the ancient Greek list of virtues directly applicable to individuals in the twenty-first century?

META-ETHICS: MORAL REALISM VERSUS ANTI-REALISM

Meta-ethics is the second strand of ethics, which contrasts with the first, normative ethics (see page 35) because it focuses on the nature of ethical propositions, proclamations, approaches and moral judgements. Whereas normative ethics is concerned with establishing a basis for the right course of action and analyzes questions such as 'What should I do?' and 'How should we live?' and in the process endorses certain ethical positions to the detriment of others, meta-ethics is concerned with questions such as 'How can we tell good from bad?' and 'What is goodness?' Meta-ethical questions can be divided into three separate areas:

- *Moral semantics* – concerned with establishing the meaning of moral terminology, or conversely proving the absence of meaning or truth value in moral statements.

- *Moral ontological questions* – which address the nature of moral judgements to attempt to establish if these judgements are universal or relative.

- *Moral epistemology* – which examines how we can support or reject moral judgements, and whether it is possible to know right from wrong.

Moral realism versus moral anti-realism

One widely held position among philosophers dating back to Plato is moral realism (or moral objectivism), i.e. there exist such things as moral facts and moral values, and that these are objective and exist alongside scientific and mathematical facts. Moral facts are independent of our perception of them or our beliefs, feelings and attitudes towards them. And moral realism makes the claim that moral propositions can be subjected to reason and logic to determine if they are true or false, and upholds the view that there are certain propositions that are always right or wrong. This has a distinct advantage when applied to moral disputes as logic decrees that two moral propositions that contradict each other cannot both be right or wrong at the same time.

One of the main criticisms of moral realism is that although it provides a means to resolve moral disputes, it provides little explanation as to how or why moral disputes arise in the first place. If humans have access to moral facts, why do moral disputes occur at all? In an attempt to resolve such anomalies, moral realism can be split into two different branches:

- *Moral absolutism* – there are absolute standards against which moral judgements can be made. This is a belief in moral facts that are always either right or wrong, and do not change according to circumstance.

- *Moral relativism* – people's moral beliefs differ from culture to culture, and so more than one moral position could be seen as being right in certain situations. For example, in some cultures capital punishment follows 'an eye for an eye' morality, whereas others argue that to take a human life is always morally wrong. Consequently, moral relativism can be either descriptive, i.e. it's the commonly held attitudes and beliefs of people within a certain culture that differ, or normative, when the moral facts differ from culture to culture.

In opposition to moral realism is moral anti-realism, the meta-ethical doctrine that there are no objective moral values. Moral anti-realism can involve either a denial that moral properties exist at all, or the acceptance that they do exist, but that their existence is mind-dependent and not objective or independent. One form of moral anti-realism is known as ethical subjectivism and argues that there are no objective moral propositions, and that ethical statements are in fact indiscriminate because they do not express undeniable truths. Instead, moral statements are made true or false by the attitudes and/or conventions of the observers, and any ethical sentence just implies an attitude, opinion, personal preference or feeling that someone holds to be true. Thus, for a statement to be considered morally right merely means that it is met with approval by the person of interest.

Ethical subjectivism also holds that judgements about human conduct are shaped by, and in many ways limited to, personal perceptions. For example, an ethical subjectivist would argue that the statement 'Hitler was evil' expresses strong disapproval for his historical atrocities that does not express that it is true (or false) that Hitler was in fact evil. Others may disagree with 'Hitler was evil' on purely moral grounds, while simultaneously agreeing with all the historical evidence and non-evaluative facts about Hitler and, by doing so, they are not making an error of judgement, merely expressing a different attitude and perception. One of the principle objections to the idea that there are no moral truths that can be objectively verified is that it places morality in an ethical vacuum where there is no difference between right and wrong, which has dangerous implications for how individuals act and societies function.

The debate between moral realism (the existence of universal moral facts) and moral anti-realism (the belief that there are no moral facts) is closely linked to key issues in theology (see Chapter 5). Philosophers such as J.L. Mackie (1917–81) have devised what is known as error theory, which they have deployed to address questions such as if God is omnibenevolent (morally perfect) why does evil exist?

Hume, the enlightened philosopher

David Hume (1711–76) was a major figure in the Scottish Enlightenment (a group of thinkers engaged with moral and political philosophy in the late eighteenth and early nineteenth centuries). His best-known work is *A Treatise on Human Nature* (1789), in which he attempted to create a 'science of man' to describe human nature, encompassing aspects of perception, identity and ethics relating to individuals and societies. Hume's ethical position was that passions, desires and sentiments are at the root of morals, not reason, arguing that 'Morals excite passions, and produce or prevent actions. Reason itself is utterly impotent in this particular. The rules of morality, therefore, are not conclusions of our reason.'

Hume's Guillotine: the is/ought problem

Hume is credited with being the first philosopher to approach what is known as the 'is/ought problem'. He observes in *Treatise* what he sees as a tendency of certain writers and philosophers, particularly when describing ethics, to switch between positive or descriptive statements relating to 'what is' (and can be empirically proved) and normative statements (what 'ought to be'). For Hume, it is not clear that there is a direct relation between positive and normative statements as, given our knowledge of how something *is*, in what sense can we argue or be informed to how it *ought* to be. The is/ought problem is known as Hume's Guillotine because it severed the often implied (but for Hume logically impossible) relationship between positive and normative statements or propositions.

APPLIED ETHICS: THEORY INTO PRACTICE

Applied ethics (the third strand of ethics) is the application of ethical theories to concrete situations in private and public life. In general, applied ethics relates to areas such as science, health care and medicine, but also to business and politics. Examples of bio-ethical dilemmas in life sciences include the use of human embryos in research, or the distribution of scarce resources in medicine and care for the sick or infirm, or ecological issues concerning pollution and the environment.

Traditionally seen as distinct from normative and meta-ethical areas, applied ethics attempts to find practical applications for the different theories. For example, pluralistic deontology is a form of normative ethics proposed by the Scottish philosopher W.D. Ross (1877–1971) in his work *The Right and The Good* (1930). He approached ethics from a consequentialist and utilitarian position by arguing that the moral worth of an action is determined by its consequence, and that there are certain duties that are always good.

Ross identified seven *prima facie* duties or accepted principles of ethics to consider when deciding a course of action in any given situation:

- *Beneficence* – the duty to help others in order to increase their pleasure and wellbeing, and negate pain and suffering or improve their character.

- *Non-maleficence* – the duty to never knowingly cause harm or distress to others through cruelty.

- *Justice* – the duty to ensure people get what they deserve in terms of fairness and equality.

- *Self-improvement* – the duty to improve ourselves in practical and spiritual ways for the benefit of ourselves and wider communities.

- *Reparation* – the duty to provide recompense and reparation to a person or situation, if wronged by the consequences of personal actions.

- *Gratitude* – the duty to show appropriate gratitude towards people for their help or if benefitting from their actions.

- *Promise-keeping/fidelity* – the duty to act according to explicit and implicit promises, including the implicit promise (see Kant's categorical imperative, page 43) to always tell the truth.

Ross does not provide a hierarchy of importance in relation to his scheme of duties, nor does he claim these are the only duties individuals should consider. One flaw in his list is that in certain circumstances and conflicts two or more *prima facie* duties may be in opposition or conflict, causing a dilemma over which duty to endorse. For example, a father may have promised to take his child to see the latest blockbuster movie when a friend calls to ask for help moving house. The friend had previously done several selfless favours and expects one in return. So the duty of gratitude conflicts with beneficence and promise-keeping.

However, Ross argued that in most situations there is always an 'absolute duty', which holds more weight than others in determining the right course of action. Given the dilemma described, most people would probably side with beneficence and gratitude (and, it could be argued, justice) and help their friend at the expense of disappointing the child and breaking a promise.How different people weigh-up the consequences of a particular decision is problematic.The contemporary American philosopher Shelly Kagan (b. 1954) argued in *The Limits of Morality* (1989) that Ross should have used the term *pro tanto*, meaning 'to an extent', to describe his reasons for duty rather than *prima facie* because 'a *pro tanto* reason has genuine weight, but nonetheless may be outweighed by other considerations ... a *prima facie* reason appears to be a reason, but may actually not be a reason at all'. Kagan's argument is that the weight of a duty depends on 'the extent' to which it correlates or conflicts with other duties in Ross's scheme, and that invoking one duty as heavier than another is a matter of judgement to provide justification and it is not necessarily absolute.

Whistle-blowers: heroes or traitors?

Many organizations and businesses draw up mission statements and codes of conduct. Similarly, governments, legislative bodies (broadly speaking, the machinery of the law) and departments of state, including health, defence, welfare and education, have codes of conduct drawn up from applied ethical models. However, these moral guidelines are often not binding in the sense of being 'set in stone'.

The postmodernist philosopher Jacques Derrida (1930–2004; see page 143) was apt, when speaking of applied ethics, that the United Nations Universal Declaration of Human Rights, first ratified in 1948 after the Second World War, has been modified and revised on numerous occasions since. This can be explained in part to shifts and changes in the global world order, developments in technology, ecology and the socio-political climate in different parts of the world. It is also, from Derrida's perspective, proof of the futility of moral laws that are binding in a prescriptive sense.

In recent times, the moral dilemmas faced by whistle-blowers exposing the moral and unethical practices of organizations and businesses has been a key point of contention for applied ethics. On one hand, whistle-blowers can be seen as heroes, standing up for the rights of individuals against monstrously bureaucratic corporations and institutions, who are doing 'wrong' under a cloud of secrecy. On the other, whistle-blowers are often portrayed as traitors or harbouring irrational or ill-founded grudges; misfits who aren't part of the collective consciousness.

A key example of this dichotomy in applied ethics is the case of former CIA operative Edward Snowden. Snowden was a former computer data analyst for the US government who copied and leaked classified information from the National Security Agency (NSA) in 2013, without authorization, to the German newspaper *Der Spiegel*. His disclosures revealed numerous global surveillance programmes, many run by the NSA and the Five Eyes Intelligence Alliance with the implicit co-operation of telecommunication companies and European governments. Snowden's revelations caused a sensation and sparked an on-going debate on the nature of privacy in the digital age, and the right of governments to 'spy' on their citizens.

3

What you need to know about

THE PHILOSOPHY OF SCIENCE

The philosophy of science is the study of the assumptions, foundations and implications of the natural sciences, e.g. biology, chemistry, physics, earth science, medicine and astronomy. A distinction is drawn between the natural sciences and social sciences – psychology, anthropology, sociology, etc. – that focus primarily on human behaviour and social structures. The principal questions in the philosophy of science include: What is science? What are the aims of science? How should we interpret and utilize the knowledge acquired through scientific study? This final question throws up ethical dilemmas surrounding how scientific knowledge is obtained and is addressed in Chapter 4.

Mathematics, rightly viewed, possesses not only truth but supreme beauty – a beauty cold and austere, like that of a sculpture.

BERTRAND RUSSELL

WHAT IS SCIENTISM?

Scientism is central to a philosophical debate on what constitutes science and it distinguishes certain areas of knowledge from pseudo-science, or purely theoretical science. Scientism – a much-maligned term in some quarters – is the general, overarching standpoint that the assumptions and methods of research of the physical and natural sciences (scientific method) are equally applicable to other areas of human knowledge, including philosophy, the humanities and the social sciences.

Logical positivism is a form of scientism that foregrounds the view that 'authentic knowledge' is scientific knowledge; theories that can be scientifically verified and can be logically or mathematically proved. Positivism argues that such knowledge can only come from the positive affirmation of theory through subjection to a strict scientific method. Traditionally, this method centres on the gathering of empirical 'evidence' by collecting data through a process of observation and experimentation, leading to the formulation and testing of hypotheses.

Aristotle – the son of a prominent Athenian physician who showed a particular aptitude for biology and uncovering the 'nature' of things – is thought to have written the first systematic treatise on the nature of scientific inquiry that encompassed observation and reasoning about the natural world. In his works *Prior Analytics* and *Posterior Analytics*, Aristotle reflects first on the aims and then the methods of inquiry into nature. His method, although not without its flaws, nonetheless contained a number of aspects considered essential to the study of science today. But while a concentration on empiricism and careful observation is at the basis of all scientific inquiry, he promoted a form of dispassionate observation and not controlled experimentation. The aim was not merely to accumulate observable facts for their own sake, because controlled experiments can lead to theories constructing their own objects and prejudged conclusions.

Aristotle uses the word '*episteme*' when he wrote about science, and this constitutes a totality of accurately arranged knowledge – the empirical facts – but what is important is how these facts are arranged and presented. So the goal of discovery, through observation, ordering and the presentation of facts, influences the methods required for a successful scientific inquiry. A further determinant is the nature of the knowledge being sought, and the function and causes related to a particular branch of knowledge.

In addition to careful observation, Aristotle's scientific method required:

- A logical system of reasoning for correctly arranging and analysing facts, but also for inferring or predicting beyond what has been gathered through observation.
- Moreover, the methods of reasoning could include deduction, prediction, comparison or analogy.

Aristotle's system outlined in *Prior Analytics* and *Posterior Analytics* (along with his repudiations of other theories of scientific methodologies and false reasoning) were collected under the title of the *Organon,* which means 'instrument' or 'tool'.

When scientific method goes wrong

Aristotle's writings on science and nature had such a profound influence upon the natural sciences, particularly during the medieval period, that some of his glaring errors were accepted more or less verbatim and remained unchallenged for centuries. *The History of Animals* (*c.* 350 BC) was Aristotle's investigation into zoology and an attempt to apply his scientific method to existing facts and the causes of the natural world.

King bee

One section of Aristotle's *The History of Animals* contains detailed observations on the life of bees. He correctly surmised that bee colonies contain three types of bees: workers, drones and a 'king'. It is the substitution of 'king' for 'queen' that has caused the most controversy and is seen by some as Aristotle's misogynistic views on women.

Aristotle was correct in his observation that bees collect material from flowers, but he believed that the flowers spawned young bees and that they were incapable of reproduction. He also believed that honey was produced from atmospheric conditions, his argument being that there are periods of the year when flowers are abundant but no honey is produced. In fact, this observation is only half wrong as atmospherics do indeed affect honey production, it was merely the pollination process that Aristotle failed to grasp.

Although *The History of Animals* contains many ground-breaking observations, particularly in marine biology, it contains several conspicuous blunders. One particularly notable mistake was Aristotle's claim that flies have fourlegs, although scholars have argued that this could have been a mistranslation that remained uncorrected.

Francis Bacon – the renaissance philosopher

Sir Francis Bacon (1561–1626) was an English philosopher, statesman, politician, lawyer and writer, and a leading figure in the English renaissance. A prolific writer, he produced philosophical works on a variety of subjects including science, theology, ethics, politics and the law. He is best remembered for his contribution to the philosophy of science and in particular for his text *Novum Organum* (meaning 'new instrument'; 1620), which formed the basis for what became known as the 'Baconian Method'.

Bacon's *Novum Organum* was an attempt to formulate a new system of scientific inquiry that was a departure from Aristotle's method, which had had a profound influence on medieval science. Whereas Aristotle's method took its logical reasoning from the use of syllogisms – a form of deductive reasoning based upon two or more related premises that are taken to be true – Bacon's method deployed 'inductive reasoning'.

Inductive reasoning is a method of reasoning in which the premises are viewed as supplying some evidence for the truth of the conclusion. While the conclusion of a deductive argument is certain, the truth of the conclusion of an inductive argument may be probable, being based upon the evidence recorded and presented. Bacon gives the example of an inquiry into the cause of a 'phenomenal nature', such as heat.

- First, the scientist makes a list (A) of all of the possible situations where heat can be found and observed.

- List B then notes conditions comparable to those in A, but where heat is not present.

- The third and final list (C) is drawn up in which the presence or absence of heat can be variable.

Bacon argues that in order to ascertain the 'form nature' (natural characteristics) of heat, a comparative analysis of all three tables will reveal that heat corresponds with all instances of List A, doesn't correspond to any instances in List B and varies in all instances to List C.

Novum Organum was influential in the historical development of the scientific method. Bacon's technique bears a resemblance to the modern scientific approach because it is grounded in experimental research and departs from Aristotle's suspicion of controlled experimentation. And Bacon's emphasis on the use of artificial conditions to provide additional observances of a phenomenon led Voltaire, among others, to hail him as 'the Father of Experimental Philosophy'. Bacon's conviction that natural philosophy must begin with the evidence of the senses was a radical departure from scientific tradition, and its resulting method of eliminative induction was one of his most lasting contributions to science and philosophy.

Bacon's development of a 'new instrument' for scientific enquiry also turned out to be fatal. After he had been disbarred from parliament following a corruption scandal, he devoted the remainder of his life to writing about and conducting scientific experiments. He died of pneumonia in 1626, possibly from spending too many hours testing meat to see if it could be preserved by being buried in compacted snow.

WHEN IS A SCIENCE A NON-SCIENCE?

One of the central questions in the philosophy of science is the argument that attempts to make a clear distinction between science and non-science or pseudo-science. In a historical sense, the main points of contention have fixed on the divide between 'pure science' and religion and theology. It may seem absurd that such a pivotal problem still rages on, still unresolved, most pertinently in the western world, but equally vociferously in other regions where religious ideology has a significant influence upon political power and social structures.

While the three-way debate between proponents of 'evolutionism', 'creationism' and 'intelligent design theory' is examined in Chapter 5, there are other areas of philosophy, including metaphysics and ethics, that have also been treated with suspicion by those advocating 'pure science'. The criteria, as we have seen from the scientific methods of Aristotle and Bacon, to establish science involves:

- The formulation of hypotheses that meet the logical criteria of contingency. That is to say, theories and ideas that are neither necessarily true nor false.

- Hypotheses that can be subjected to a process capable of proving them false.

- Hypotheses that are testable to establish that under certain circumstances they can be deemed true or false.

- The gathering of empirical evidence through observation, which can subsequently be analysed through the rigours of logical, scientific methodology.

Empiricism and, later, positivism and logical positivism, grounded science with a very disciplined, quasi-obsession with observation, and campaigned for a systematic reduction of all human knowledge to logical, mathematical and scientific foundations. This perspective was very much to the detriment of other disciplines and areas of philosophy, including metaphysics, theology, spiritualism and the social sciences, as they were deemed to be 'non-science' on the grounds that they were non-observational.

This philosophical viewpoint is known as *verificationism* and decrees that only statements or propositions that are empirically verifiable (i.e. through the senses) are cognitively meaningful, or can be shown to be logically true. However, the logical positivism project found many detractors, largely because verificationism seemed to be, in a sense, closing more doors to human knowledge than it was opening.

Karl Popper and scepticism

Karl Popper (1902–94) was born into a wealthy family in Vienna where he studied philosophy, psychology and mathematics at the local university. As a student he became interested in Marxism and was a member of the Social Democratic Workers Party, an organization that was then fervently Marxist.

Vienna was one of the centres of European intellectuals

in the 1920s with pioneering work in psychology by the likes of Sigmund Freud and Alfred Adler, and in philosophy and logic by a group of academics who formed the Vienna Circle. It was the fashion for logical positivism proposed by the Vienna Circle, with a concentration on the natural sciences, which formed the starting point for Popper's ideas about scientific methods.

By the 1930s, Popper had become disillusioned with Marxism and began to distance himself from logical positivism. In 1934, he published *The Logic of Scientific Discovery*, which challenged logical positivism and scientific methods that were based upon inductive reasoning. For Popper, scientific knowledge was not verified through confirming a relationship between hypotheses and evidence. He argued that the classical approach to science, which entailed the formation of hypotheses followed by confirmation of theory through repeated experiment and observation, was flawed. For example, a scientist has a hypothesis that Crohn's disease can lead to anaemia. The scientist observes a sample of patients diagnosed with the disease and all develop varying degrees of anaemia, and so he concludes that the relationship between his original hypotheses and the evidence he has compiled has confirmed his theory.

Popper's argument was that, in this example, it would only take one or two patients to not develop anaemia to disprove the original hypothesis, and therefore no amount of observation can ever actually provide absolute proof beyond doubt. This switching of emphasis was, for Popper, the only way for science to progress – not by proving what seems to be confirmed through observation, but by unearthing instances when a hypotheses or theory is false. Popper named this process 'falsificationism'.

To return to the example of Crohn's disease and patients developing anaemia, although a large number of the sample developed the subsidiary illness, several didn't. The conclusion therefore is that there is a probability, or it is not uncommon, for Crohn's patients to develop anaemia because the evidence is 'well-corroborated'. Popper argued that too much science confuses 'corroboration' with confirmation in the search for 'truth', and that the actual truth of a hypothesis relies on the instances where there is disagreement between the theory and the evidence.

Thomas Kuhn and the paradigm shift

The American physicist and philosopher Thomas Kuhn (1922–96) caused a sensation in the long-running science versus non-science debate with the publication in 1962 of his book *The Structure of Scientific Revolutions*. Kuhn was born in Cincinnati and studied physics and mathematics at Harvard University, gaining his PhD in 1949 under the Nobel Prize-winning physicist John Van Vleck.

Kuhn then taught philosophy and the history of science at the University of California, Berkeley. It was during this period that he began to develop his ideas on the development of scientific knowledge through history.

He coined the phrase 'normal science' to describe traditional approaches to scientific method, i.e. testing hypotheses through observation to formulate and provide the confirmation of a theory. However, Kuhn also defined normal science as a process of problem solving within a central paradigm. He argued that scientific knowledge never progressed in a linear fashion, but rather consists of a series of central paradigms that remain the norm, via a consensus of the scientific community, until a problem or puzzle becomes insurmountable. At this point the central paradigm 'shifts' in emphasis and is replaced by a new paradigm with new puzzles to be solved. A basic example is the assertion of Nicolaus Copernicus (1473–1543) that the sun is at the centre of the solar system and not the earth.

Kuhn outlined three distinct stages that scientific knowledge undergoes:

- He termed the first 'prescience' – an ingenious pun on the Latin word '*praescientia*', meaning 'foreknowledge' and 'pre-science' (i.e. before science). Prescience has no central paradigm, to return to our model of Copernicus and the movement of celestial objects; this period notes that the sun shifts position but there is no model to explain why.

- Normal science then observes the movements of the sun and determines that the sun is revolving around the earth, and this becomes the central paradigm. However, over time the normal science conducted by astronomers runs into difficulties as not all the puzzles – here concerning the movement of other planets – fit the paradigm.

- Copernicus's 1534 publication of *De revolutionibus orbium coelestium* (*On the Revolutions of the Celestial Spheres*) caused a paradigm shift by replacing the old paradigm with a new central paradigm, replete with a new set of puzzles to solve.

Kuhn argued that a new paradigm is accepted mainly because it has a superior ability to solve problems that arise in the process of normal science, and pseudoscience or non-science can then be defined by a failure to provide explanations within such a paradigm. This argument can be seen as a refutation of Popper's falsification theory, as failure to solve puzzles within an accepted paradigm is not seen as a failure of method or inability to confirm hypotheses, merely a failure of the researcher, and therefore does not refute the viability of the central paradigm.

Paradigm shifts do not dispense with the knowledge detected from previous paradigms, they integrate knowledge into new paradigms.

In this way, science progresses not just by gradually building on the works of the past, as had always been assumed, but by a series of revolutions in which the ways of thinking in the scientific community are changed completely. *The Structure of Scientific Revolutions* was hugely popular, both in academic circles and with the public at large, and is one of the great popular science texts of the twentieth century.

THE ANARCHY OF SCIENCE

Paul Feyerabend (1924–94) was born in Vienna and studied philosophy and the philosophy of science under Karl Popper at the London School of Economics. Feyerabend had originally been granted a scholarship by the British Council to work with Popper's *bête noire,* Ludwig Wittgenstein (1889–1951), but Wittgenstein's sudden death from cancer in 1951 resulted in Feyerabend moving to London. Early in his academic career, Feyerabend was influenced by Popper's theories of 'falsificationism' (see page 72), but after taking up a position at the University of California, Berkeley, he developed a radical theory of the philosophy of science, influenced in part by the ideas of his colleague Thomas Kuhn.

In his ground-breaking and provocative book *Against Method* (1975), Feyerabend argued that science does not occupy a special place in terms of either its logic or method, and that there is no method within the history of scientific practice which has not been violated at some point in advancing scientific knowledge, so that any claim to special authority made by scientists cannot be upheld.

Feyerabend was critical of any guiding method that aimed to evaluate the quality of scientific theories by comparing them to known facts. Expanding upon Kuhn's ideas about paradigm shifts and scientific revolutions, Feyerabend argued that previous theories could influence natural interpretations of observed phenomena. Scientific methodology makes implied assumptions when relating scientific theories to facts that are determined through observation. The problem for Feyerbend is that these assumptions then need to be altered in order to make the new theory compatible with new observations. This view is best summed up by Feyerabend's maxim that in the history of science there is 'change' but not necessarily 'progress'.

Feyerabend advocated an anarchistic approach to science that encompassed areas traditionally thought of as pseudo-science, such as supernatural phenomena, astrology and the occult. It was his belief that the strict empirical structure of scientific methods stunted creativity and as such was a hindrance to the development of real knowledge.

Feyerabend: the idle philosopher

He was not a man who embraced the Protestant work ethic. In his posthumously published and aptly titled *Killing Time* (1995), Feyerabend viewed his academic career as simply a means to earn money and kill time between engaging in more pleasurable and worthwhile pursuits, most notably cooking, eating, drinking and opera. In 1974, he became a professor at the University of Sussex. At this point he was a global academic celebrity and his Sussex lectures (when the unwilling philosopher actually bothered to turn up and give them) became legendary and were attended by hundreds, including large numbers of non-students. But despite his popularity with the students he resigned after just two months because the university insisted he work twelve hours a week. 'One lecture a week and the rest student tutorials was much too much like hard work,' he noted. Fittingly, the German word '*feyerabend*' is now commonly used to mean the moment when work finishes or the end of the allotted working day.

The tower argument

The key example of the influence of dubious natural interpretations in science, that Feyerabend objected to in *Against Method*, was the 'tower argument'. Since the time of Aristotle, physics had followed a geocentric view of the organization of the cosmos: the Earth was in a fixed position, and the sun and stars revolved around it. The publication in 1543 of *On the Revolutions of the Celestial Spheres* by Nicolaus Copernicus had introduced a heliocentric model of the cosmos, placing the sun at the centre of the universe. Copernicus' theory was controversial at the time and fell foul of the Catholic Church, which believed that placing the sun at the centre of the universe contradicted the scriptures. For example, Psalm 104:5 in the Bible states: 'The Lord set the earth on its foundations; it can never be moved.'

The tower argument was one of the main objections against the theory of a moving Earth. Aristotelians assumed that the Earth is stationary because when a stone is dropped from a tower it lands directly beneath it. According to current observation of objects in motion, if the Earth moved while the stone was falling, the stone would have been 'left behind' and would fall at a diagonal angle. However, as the stone falls perpendicular to the tower and lands at the base, Aristotelians took this as evidence that the Earth did not move. Galileo Galilei (1564–1642) was an early supporter of Copernicus' ideas and soon found himself in trouble with the Catholic authorities. However, despite having his works suppressed by the Inquisition, Feyerabend argues that Galileo, rather than trying to fit his observations into an accepted model, turned the whole methodology on its head in the name of scientific truth.

4

What you need to know about

THE PHILOSOPHY OF POLITICS AND POWER

Political philosophy is the study of fundamental questions concerning government and the state, and encompasses ideas about liberty, justice and the law. Common discussions in political philosophy relate to the roles and responsibilities of individuals and groups within societies, and ask questions such as: What is a government? Are governments necessary? How is political power legitimized? What basic rights and freedoms should a government protect?

However, the philosophy of power is less concerned with practical applications of political systems and state organization, and it takes a more theoretical approach to how power functions in societies.

As with most areas of philosophy, the tradition of western political philosophy can be traced back to Ancient Greece, where city-states experimented and developed many forms of political organization. The term 'democracy', for example (an often misused, misappropriated and problematic concept), is derived from the Greek '*dēmokratía*', which was devised from the word '*dēmos*' ('people') and '*kratos*' ('rule'); so democracy literally means rule of the people. Among the most significant classical works of political philosophy are Plato's *The Republic*, Aristotle's *Politics*, Thomas Hobbes' *Leviathan* (1651) and Niccolò Machiavelli's *The Prince* (1532).

PLATO'S REPUBLIC: THE 'JUST' MAN/'JUST' STATE

The most famous and probably the most influential of Plato's works is contained in a series of Socratic dialogues, known collectively as *The Republic*. Socrates discusses with various prominent Athenians and friends, most notably Plato's brothers, the meaning of the concept of justice and how it applies to individuals and wider society. Socrates examines a series of questions such as 'Do men behave justly because it is intrinsically good for them to do so?' and 'Is justice therefore a good thing as and of itself?' How, ultimately, do we define justice and once we have that definition is the just man happier and more righteous than the unjust man?

Plato/Socrates outlines a three-part hierarchical structure of the human soul, which they believe is immortal but masked by the material world of objects:

- At the top is the rational and intellectual part of the soul seeking truth, knowledge and understanding, and the basis for philosophical practice.

- Beneath is a spirited part of the soul, which is driven by notions of honour and duty and provokes passionate feelings of anger, indignation and righteousness.

- Third is the appetitive part of the soul, seeking to satisfy our basic requirements and needs, but which can be corrupted by lust and desires. For an individual to have a 'just' soul, the three parts must exist in a harmonious power relationship with one another.

The rational part of the soul must have dominance and determinism, supported by the spirited part, and the appetitive part must submit to wherever reason and judgement lead.

Plato then suggests that a just soul is analogous with a just or ideal society (i.e. the republic of the title) and, just as the soul contains a hierarchical structure of three parts, so does society. At the top are 'the guardians', whom Plato defines as 'Philosopher-Kings', the custodians of wisdom and reason with the best interests of the people at heart. The guardians are supported by 'auxiliaries', or 'soldiers', whose job is to protect and support values of honour and duty through strength and loyalty. And at the bottom are the artisans or 'producers', corresponding to the appetitive element of the soul, e.g. the craftsmen and workers. A 'just society' exists when the relationship between the three parts maintains a harmony of balance, and each group must perform its requisite role – and only that role – and must maintain the appropriate position of power in relation to the other groups.

So, the 'Philosopher-Kings' are responsible for decision and rule-making, the 'auxiliaries' must support the rulers' principles and the 'producers' must be limited to exercising the talents and skills nature granted them to provide for society's basic needs for survival (food, shelter, clothing, etc.). In this sense, for Plato, justice is a principle of inter-related specialization: a code that requires each person to fulfil the societal role that nature has bequeathed them, and not to interfere in business beyond their defined remit.

As Plato writes: 'To do one's own business and not to be a busybody is justice.' Or, put simply, in the 'just state' each class and each individual has a specific set of duties and roles, a set of obligations to the community, which, if everyone fulfils them, will result in a harmonious society. When a person follows his duties, he receives whatever credit and reward he deserves, but if he fails in his role, or oversteps his mark, he is appropriately punished.

ARISTOTLE'S *POLIS* – A UTOPIA OF HAPPINESS

At the conclusion of *Nicomachean Ethics*, Aristotle argues that any analysis of individual ethics naturally extends into the ethics of communities and public life, the realm of the political as 'man is a political animal'. In his work *Politics*, Aristotle analyzes the different constitutions and methods of governance of what he terms the *polis,* or Greek city-states such as his native Athens. The term 'politics' literally means matters concerning the *polis* (city). For Aristotle, the *polis* is the most prominent form of political and social association, and differs from other forms of community partnerships such as households or villages in terms of size and scope. The aim of the *polis* is to encourage its citizens to live a life of quality and virtue, for public life takes precedence over private affairs.

The *Politics* begins by reviewing and analyzing forms of constitution and political organization. Aristotle criticises Plato's *Republic*, interpreting Plato's central tenet to be that citizens of the *polis* should share in common as much as possible, including wives, children and property. The aim of Aristotle's communities is to accomplish unity, but Aristotle argues that cities by nature are places of plurality as different people make different contributions, fulfil different roles and fit into separate social classes. This plurality is necessary for cities to function, and to preserve autonomy and self-sufficiency. He concludes that past and contemporary cities, and theories of political organization, had not achieved an ideal of form or purpose.

According to Aristotle, there are six different categories of city with related constitutional structures; three that are positive and good and three that are negative and bad. The positive are what he terms *politeia*, the enshrined constitutional rights of citizens within a city-state, an aristocracy and a monarchy. The negative are democracy, oligarchy and tyranny. He also argues that tyranny is an inadequate form of government because it concentrates only on the interests of the ruling class, that oligarchy is centred only on the interests of the wealthy and that democracy represents a form of mob-rule:

> For tyranny is a kind of monarchy which has in view the interest of the monarch only; oligarchy has in view the interest of the wealthy; democracy, of the needy: none of them the common good of all. Tyranny, as I was saying, is monarchy exercising the rule of a master over the political society; oligarchy is when men of property have the government in their hands; democracy, the opposite, when the indigent, and not the men of property, are the rulers.
>
> ARISTOTLE – *POLITICS* BOOK II

For Aristotle, healthy political organization should be formulated on the principles of distributive justice, which decrees that equal people should be treated equally and unequal people are treated unequally. People should be valued according to the contributions they make to the collective life of the citizens of the city. Aristotle argues that although a constitutional government (*politiea),* with its set of sovereign laws, remains the ideal form of political organization, a monarch, if he/she holds the interests of their citizens as inviolable, may in some situations be equally effective.

After reviewing various forms of government, Aristotle concludes that effective political organization benefits from a strong, educated middle class that can mediate between the conflicting interests of the aristocratic rich and the 'indigent' poor. He divides the duties of government into deliberative functions (planning), legal matters concerning the rule of law, and executive decision-making for the good of the citizens as a whole. Constitutions fall when a large faction opposed to the ruling class rises up and attempts to overthrow the status quo. Aristotle cautions that excluding minorities bereft of power is folly, and that governments should act with moderation, prudence and respect towards all to ensure stability in the city.

When picturing his ideal *polis* Aristotle declares that the ultimate objective of the government should be to help facilitate each citizen to achieve happiness, virtue and quality of life. Virtue can be attained through the free exercise of speculative reasoning and contemplation. Cities should be kept to a manageable size, large enough to be self-sufficient but small enough for the citizens to each take an active part in the city's affairs. Furthermore, citizens should share and participate in military service, matters of government, religious service and have a stake in land ownership. But Aristotle didn't believe that citizens should be expected to fulfil the role of Plato's 'producers', with crafts and food production being the duty of non-citizens.

> The citizens must not lead the life of mechanics or tradesmen, for such a life is ignoble, and inimical to virtue. Neither must they be farmers, since leisure

> is necessary both for the development of virtue and the performance of political duties.
>
> ARISTOTLE - *POLITICS* BOOK VII

And, finally, there's Aristotle's concept of 'leisure' – a programme of education encompassing reading and writing, philosophy, art, gymnastics and music for the purpose of promoting quality of life, virtue and moral goodness.

HOBBES *LEVIATHAN* AND THE SOCIAL CONTRACT

Thomas Hobbes (1588–1679) was born in Malmesbury, Wiltshire, allegedly on the eve of the arrival of the Spanish Armada, a claim Hobbes was fond of making, although the Armada actually set sail over a month after his birth. The son of a local vicar, he was educated first by the church and private tutors before attending the University of Oxford. A talented scholar, his works range from ancient history – in 1628 he produced the first English translation of Thucydides' *History of the Peloponnesian War* – to geometry, science and theology. But it is in the area of political philosophy that Hobbes is most revered, particularly for his seminal work *Leviathan* (1651), written at the height of the English Civil War.

In *Leviathan*, Hobbes' intention was to apply scientific

principles to an analysis of human behaviour in order to draw some conclusions around the legitimacy of political organization. Hobbes was at heart a materialist who was acquainted with Galileo and other prominent European intellectuals of his day, and who took a mechanistic view of the world – a world made up of perpetual motion, driven by positive and negative forces. Central to Hobbes' philosophy is man in a 'state of nature', unencumbered by social organization and driven by self-interest and doomed to 'a war of all against all'.

> In such condition, there is no place for industry; because the fruit thereof is uncertain: and consequently no culture of the earth; no navigation, nor use of the commodities that may be imported by sea; no commodious building; no instruments of moving, and removing, such things as require much force; no knowledge of the face of the earth; no account of time; no arts; no letters; no society; and which is worst of all, continual fear, and danger of violent death; and the life of man, solitary, poor, nasty, brutish, and short.
>
> THOMAS HOBBES – *LEVIATHAN*

Thomas Hobbes and the philosopher's stone

Towards the end of his life, Hobbes invited friends to come up with suggestions for his epitaph. Apparently the one he thought most appropriate to be carved on his gravestone was 'This is the true philosopher's stone', but for some reason it was not used. Ring a bell? *The Philosopher's Stone* became J.K. Rowling's title of the second volume in the phenomenally popular Harry Potter series.

In order to avoid this state of turmoil and lawlessness, Hobbes argues that civil societies are formed around 'a social contract'. This is a consensus agreement whereby the subjects of a dominion accede to the rule of an absolute monarch in return for peace and protection. However, the protection of their subjects is the highest duty of the monarch and corresponds to their obligations within the social contract.

Given the unstable political climate in England at the time of writing, it is not surprising that *Leviathan* was controversial. The loyalists disliked Hobbes' rejection of the traditional divine right of monarchs, the view that God appoints kings and queens to rule. Parliamentarians were also incensed at the idea of the monarchy ruling unchecked and unhindered by a legislative apparatus. Nonetheless, *Leviathan* holds an important place in the history of political philosophy, and its notion of a social contract to bind society together was further elaborated on by Hobbes' contemporaries, the philosophers John Locke (1632–1704) and Jean-Jacques Rousseau (1712–78).

MACHIAVELLI'S *THE PRINCE*

Niccolò di Bernardo dei Machiavelli (1469–1527) was an Italian politician, diplomat, playwright and poet responsible for one of the seminal works of Renaissance political philosophy. His best-known work, *Il Principe* (*The Prince*; 1532) was constructed as a sort of guidebook on how to effectively rule, with one subversive aspect: Machiavelli obliquely questions the legitimacy of hereditary succession of power and suggests ways in which 'a new prince' can seize and maintain a stable city-state.

In order to maintain power, a traditional monarch/ruler granted power by birthright is, in Machiavelli's view, required to carefully balance the interests of various dominant institutions – the church, aristocracy, judiciary, etc. – within the society he presides over. The new prince is required to find a form of political activity that provides stability for the state, while retaining and maintaining ultimate authority. Machiavelli argues that public and private morality must be implicitly judged as separate in order for the prince to effectively rule.

The suggestion, therefore, is that the social benefits of stability and security are achievable despite the immoral actions of rulers. In short, the ends (stability and security) justify the means (often dubiously ethical and violent actions). As a result, a ruler must be concerned not only with reputation, but must also be positively willing to act immorally at key times. For Machiavelli, it was more helpful for rulers to be feared than to be unconditionally loved, as fear provides stability through threat of reprisal, repercussion and punishment.The loved ruler retains power only through obligation. Machiavelli therefore argued for the legitimacy of the need – in certain circumstances for the methodical use of violence or deceit, including extermination of entire noble families – in order to subjugate any challenge to the prince's authority.

> *It is much safer to be feared than loved, when of the two either must be dispensed with.*
>
> NICCOLÒ DI BERNARDO DEI MACHIAVELLI –
> *THE PRINCE*

Machiavelli's pivotal view is that proud and intractable principles can lead to weak and ineffective government. This premise is especially true with respect to personal virtue. In a classical, Aristotelian view, virtues should be admired and respected as and of themselves, *a priori*. However, for a ruler (the 'prince') to act in agreement with personal virtue is often unfavourable to the stability of the state. Equally, certain vices may be frowned upon, but brutal actions are occasionally necessary to the benefit of the state; why is war ever justified under such terms? Machiavelli follows this argument and develops the idea that procuring the favour of the population is the best way to maintain power. Thus, the appearance of virtue may be more important than true virtue, which, under certain circumstances and in the judgement of history, may be proved false.

The Marxist philosopher and critic Antonio Gramsci (1891–1937) drew great inspiration from *The Prince*, maintaining that Machiavelli wasn't writing for the ruling class because it already knew how to impose 'hegemonic' structures (i.e. methods of suppressing their subjects via dominant ideological forms). He said that Machiavelli was trying to educate the disenfranchised and dispossessed about the structures of power, and how it operates on individuals and communities.

Is *The Prince* a satire?

Machiavelli wrote *The Prince* during a time of severe political conflict in his native state of Florence. In his day-job as diplomat and politician, he saw the violent brutality of his paymasters, Cesare Borgia (1475–1507) and his father, Pope Alexander VI (1431–1503). Although considered as a guidebook for would-be despots and an analysis of how political power operates in sovereign states and dominions, some commentators have suggested that *The Prince* may actually be an elaborate joke and satire. Jean-Jacques Rousseau notably argued that *The Prince* should be read as a work of political fiction and parody in the eighteenth century. In contemporary times, the political philosophers Leo Strauss (1899–1973) and Harvey Mansfield (b. 1932) have both argued that *The Prince* can be read as a work of thoughtful, comical irony.

FOUCAULT ON POWER AND KNOWLEDGE

Michel Foucault was a French philosopher, historian and social scientist associated with the postmodernism movement of European intellectuals that flourished in the late 1960s and 70s. His work centred largely on how power functions in society, and marked a departure from traditional philosophical analysis because he was attempting to unearth the forms of power operating discretely in state institutions, such as prisons, hospitals and educational establishments. Foucault rejected labels such as 'postmodernism' and even 'philosopher', preferring to see himself as a 'historian of ideas', and viewed power as something diffuse and embodied. 'Power is everywhere,' he wrote, underpinning knowledge and discourse to create 'regimes of truth'.

Foucault challenged the traditional idea that power is wielded by people or groups via certain acts or policies of domination or coercion, seeing power instead as dispersed and pervasive. As 'power is everywhere' and 'comes from everywhere', Foucault argued, it is subjected to a constant process of flux and negotiation which constitutes a form of 'meta-power' that pervades society. Foucault uses the term 'power' (knowledge) to signify that power is constituted through accepted forms of knowledge, scientific understanding and 'truth'.

Foucault argued that 'regimes of truth' resulted from scientific discourse and institutional practices that are constantly reinforced and redefined through the education system, the media, and opposing political and economic discourses and ideologies. Power operates as boundaries that enable and constrain individual possibilities for action, and on individuals' comparative capacity to recognize and shape these boundaries. However, Foucault also recognized that power is not necessarily a negative, coercive or repressive phenomenon that suppresses individuals' freedom, but can also be a necessary, productive and positive force in society. In *Truth and Power* (1991), a posthumously published collection of essays, papers and interviews, Foucault writes:

> We must cease once and for all to describe the effects of power in negative terms: it 'excludes', it 'represses', it 'censors', it 'abstracts', it 'masks', it 'conceals'. In fact, power produces; it produces reality; it produces domains of objects and rituals of truth. The individual and the knowledge that may be gained of him belong to this production.

In this sense, power and knowledge can be seen as a principle source of social discipline and conformity. In the 1960s, Foucault produced a series of historical works analyzing the development of administrative systems and social services in eighteenth-century Europe. *Madness and Civilisation* (1961) traced historical social attitudes and policies towards mental illness from the renaissance to the age of reason in the late seventeenth century. *The Birth of the Clinic* (1963) outlined the development of the medical profession and the creation of clinics and hospitals, and *Discipline and Punish* (1975) analyzed the creation of prisons and penal systems. Foucault argued in all three works that the discourses and structures underpinning these social services come together to form 'disciplinary technologies' through which power is diffused. Their systems of surveillance and assessment no longer required the traditional feudal exercise of sovereign acts of violence or force to coerce and repress, as people became conditioned to discipline themselves and follow accepted norms of behaviour.

Foucault was particularly absorbed by various methods of power and control, such as:

- Prison surveillance apparatus and Jeremy Bentham's development in the eighteenth century of the 'panopticon'.
- School discipline structures. Systems for the administration and control of populations.

- The promotion of norms about bodily conduct, including sex.

Foucault also drew upon psychology, medicine and criminology in order to define what constitutes norms of behaviour and deviance in the eyes of society. For Foucault, physical bodies are subjugated and made to behave in certain ways, as a microcosm of social control of the wider population, through what he called 'bio-power'. Disciplinary and bio-power combine to create discourses and discursive practices around what is accepted in society and what is excluded or repressed.

One of the main aspects of Foucault's notion of power is that in a sense it transcends the normal transparent exercise of political power. Foucault sees power as an everyday, socialized and embodied phenomenon, yet at the same time elusive and often removed from our perception of how it is operating to such an extent that individuals readily conform to norms of behaviour without the need of wilful coercion.

Foucault, however, did not argue that social conditioning couldn't be challenged and he believed in possibilities for action and resistance. He was an active social and political commentator and one-time member of the French Communist Party – and a prominent gay-rights activist – who saw a role for the 'organic intellectual' in social and political struggles. One key aspect of Foucault's ideas on political action concerned the capabilities and methods through which we identify and analyze socialized norms and constraints. For Foucault, to challenge power effectively did not entail unearthing 'absolute truth' – which is merely a socially constructed form of power – but 'of detaching the power of truth from the forms of hegemony, social, economic, and cultural, within which it operates at the present time'. In order for power to function it requires two aspects: a discourse (or discursive practice) and an institution, social or political. However, alternative discourses can spring up in opposition:

> Discourses are not once and for all subservient to power or raised up against it … We must make allowances for the complex and unstable process whereby a discourse can be both an instrument and an effect of power, but also a hindrance, a stumbling point of resistance and a starting point for an opposing strategy. Discourse transmits and produces power; it reinforces it, but also undermines and exposes it, renders it fragile and makes it possible to thwart.
>
> MICHEL FOUCAULT – *TRUTH AND POWER* (1991)

5

What you need to know about

THE PHILOSOPHY OF RELIGION

The philosophical study of religion examines arguments concerning the nature and existence of God, the ethical implications of religious commitments, the relationship between faith, reason, experience and tradition, and 'the problem of evil'. The philosophy of religion also tackles other branches of philosophy, including metaphysics, ethics and epistemology, the philosophy of science and even, to some extent, the philosophy of language.

The term 'philosophy of religion' was first coined in the nineteenth century as an attempt to set up a separate discipline distinct from traditional theology. Theology, or religious philosophy, is, by definition, concerned with the critical study of the nature of God and religious belief systems. Given that most of these systems take the existences of a god or gods as axiomatic, theology is accountable to a particular religious ideological framework, which its reflections seek to justify and support. Whereas the philosophy of religion asks questions such as 'Are there reasons to believe God exists?' and 'Does God have a knowable nature?', theology starts from the position that the existence of God is self-evident.

One aspect of the philosophy of religion, however, is that it proliferates 'isms' to describe different forms and aspects of religious belief such as theism, monotheism, deism and pantheism, all with different sub-branches and variations.

THE ULTIMATE REALITY OF 'ISMS'

At the centre of religious belief and value systems lies the concept of the ultimate reality – a force or power that is supreme, final and fundamentally underpins everything in existence. Religions differ in their conceptions of how this ultimate reality acts or is grounded and manifests itself. 'Theism' is the broad belief that there exists a supreme being in the universe, which is transcendent and omniscient (all knowing), omnipresent (all seeing), omnibenevolent (all loving and virtuous) and omnipotent (all powerful).

The word 'theism' derives from the Greek '*theos*' or '*theoi*' (meaning 'god') and was first used by the English theologian and philosopher Ralph Cudworth (1617–88). In his work *The True Intellectual System of the Universe* (1678), Cudworth writes that theism is the commonly held belief 'that a perfectly conscious understanding being, or mind, existing of itself from eternity, was the cause of all other things'. A fervent opponent of Thomas Hobbes, Cudworth coined the term to contrast with trends in philosophy that he believed were promoting atheism.

Within theism there are two distinct strands: monotheism and polytheism. Monotheism promotes the view that there is only one God, as believed by the major Abrahamic faiths of Judaism, Christianity and Islam. Abrahamic religions – believed to derive from the prophet Abraham in different holy texts and interpretations – are examples of exclusive monotheism, i.e. the view that one God exists and that the worship of other gods is false. In contrast, inclusive monotheism argues that there is only one God, and that the existence of God in different forms across religions is just the same God by another name. All monotheistic religions are based on the belief that God is ontologically independent, that is to say, God does not require a physical and objective manifestation in the world in order to exist.

Polytheism is the belief in the existence of multiple gods, often related to natural phenomena. Polytheistic religions were especially prevalent pre-Christianity in the religions of Ancient Egypt, Greece and Rome, and in pagan religions of northern Europe. Polytheistic religions practiced today include some strands of Hinduism, traditional Chinese religions and the Japanese rituals of Shinto.

THE EXISTENCE OF GOD PART 1

The Archbishop of Canterbury gets the ball rolling

One of the first arguments for the ontological independence of God was proposed by the Benedictine monk and theologian Anselm of Canterbury (1033–1109) in his 1078 work *Proslogion*. He defined God as 'that than which nothing greater can be thought' and argued that this being must exist in the mind, even in the minds of atheists who deny the existence of God, because the idea of an ultimate being must exist in order to deny it exists. Anselm argued therefore that if the greatest possible being exists in the mind, it must also exist in reality. Anselm also suggested that even if it only exists in the mind, then it is possible to imagine an even greater being existing, one which exists both in the mind and in reality but is ontologically independent of our perceptions.

Anselm's argument was famously refuted by another eleventh-century Bendictine monk, Gaunilo of Tours. In his work *On Behalf of the Fool*, Gaunilo tests the logic of Anselm's argument by proposing the existence of a perfect 'Lost Island':

- The Lost Island is an island of which no greater can be conceived.
- It is greater to exist in reality than merely as an idea.
- If the Lost Island does not exist in reality, one can conceive of an even greater island that does exist.
- Therefore, the Lost Island exists in reality.

Gaunilo's objection is therefore that as the Lost Island doesn't exist, the logic used to assert its existence is flawed. If the logic is flawed in the case of the Lost Island, it must also be flawed in the case of God existing – both in thought and in reality. Anselm responded by pointing out that his own definition of God is of 'that than which nothing greater can be thought' and so his argument can only be applied to the supreme power of God, and not to islands (or anything else in the universe that God created).

In fairness to Anselm, his argument was intended to be a personal meditation/observation on how he came to understand the existence of God and not, as Kant later proposed, an early attempt to apply ontological logic to the question of the existence of God. Unfortunately for Anselm, he opened a philosophical can of worms that is still raging nearly a thousand years later.

THE EXISTENCE OF GOD PART 2

St Thomas Aquinas' five proofs

St Thomas Aquinas was a Dominican priest, theologian and philosopher. Known in scholastic circles by his nickname 'Doctor Angelicus' (i.e. the Angelic Doctor), he is generally considered to be one of the most influential Christian philosophers through his life-long project to synthesize Christian theology with the philosophical reasoning of Aristotle. Aquinas' two most famous works were *Summa Contra Gentiles* (*c.* 1259–65), which was written to aid early Christian missionaries, and *Summa Theologiae* (*c.* 1265–74) – a type of course book for young monks entering the church and studying theology. *Summa Theologiae* contains what is known in theological and philosophical circles as 'The Five Proofs' (or *quinque viae*) for the existence of God. In contrast to Anselm of Canterbury's 'ontological argument', which is centred on the concept of

God, St Thomas' proofs draw upon Aristotle's method of reasoning concerning our experience and observations of the world. The five proofs in order are:

- 'The argument from motion'. Taking his cue from his reading of Aristotle, Aquinas concludes from common observation that objects in the universe are in motion. It follows that whatever is in motion now was moved by some other object or force and that object or force, in turn, was moved by another object of force. Nothing can move itself. If every object in motion had a 'mover', then the first object in motion also needed a 'mover' – the unmoved mover that started motion. Aquinas concludes that the 'unmoved mover' must be God.

- An expansion of the arguments above to examine the causation of the existence of things. We can observe things in the world that are caused or created by other things. Nothing can be the cause of itself or created from nothing, and there can't be an endless process of causation and creation without an uncaused starting point. This 'first cause' must be God.

- A distinction between what Aquinas terms as contingent, or possible, beings and necessary beings.

For contingent beings or objects, there was a time when they didn't exist (before they came into being) and there will be a time also when they cease to exist. However, it cannot be possible for everything to be contingent, as this suggests there was a time when there was nothing, and will be again. Therefore, there must be a necessary being that exists for all contingent beings and this necessary being must be God.

- Called 'the argument from degrees of perfection', Aquinas observes the human capacity to evaluate the quality of things in the universe. When we rate one painting more beautiful than another, or one person more virtuous than another, and these judgements are made by grading the quality against a notion of perfection. Although we have certain standards of how things and people should be, we could not develop those standards unless there were some being that is perfect in every way. The perfect being against which all qualities are judged must be God.

- Aquinas' final proof forms the basis for what is known as 'the argument from intelligent design'. He starts from the position that all natural things in the universe are designed for a purpose, e.g. birds' wings to aid flight, ears to process sounds. Therefore,

Aquinas and the 'angelic girdle'

Apparently Aquinas' family locked him in a tower in a bid to prevent him becoming a Dominican friar, rather than a Benedictine abbot – a much more prestigious role. While there, a prostitute was sent to his room to break his weakness for lustful temptation. A horrified Aquinas chased her away with a smouldering log from the fire. He then used the same log to draw the cross on the wall of his room and knelt in prayer before it. Immediately, two angels of purity appeared and placed an 'angelic girdle' around his waist. From that day on, he was immune to lustful thoughts or actions, and it is this 'holy purity' that is deemed the key to St Thomas and his great theological intellect – and the angelic girdle is worn by monks today as a sign and a prayer for holy purity, and inspired the expression 'chastity belt' to protect against sexual desire.

Aquinas concludes, if everything is designed for a purpose or end it cannot have evolved by chance and must have been designed by an intelligent designer – and that must be God. This last proof is known as 'The Teleological Argument'. Teleology is the study of purpose, ends, and goals in natural processes.

William Paley's watchmaker argument

William Paley (1743–1805) was an English clergyman and philosopher best known for his protractedly titled *Natural Theology or Evidences of the Existence and Attributes of the Deity collected from the Appearances of Nature* (1802). In it he presents a teleological argument in the form of a hypothetical anecdote known as 'the watchmaker analogy'.

Paley argues that if he was walking across a heath and were to step on a stone and ask how the stone came to be there, he would most likely conclude it had always been there. However, if he was walking across the heath and were to find a watch, he would not assume that it had got there by chance. Paley then draws an analogy between the complexity of the watch and the complexity of the natural world and argues that the world exhibits similar, if not superior, intricacy: 'Every indication of contrivance, every manifestation of design, which existed in the watch, exists in the works of nature; with the difference, on the side of nature, of being greater or more, and that in a degree which exceeds all computation.' Therefore, Paley surmises, since 'like' causes resemble 'like' effects, and both the watch and the natural world show signs of complex and intelligent mechanisms, both have been designed by an 'intelligent designer'; the watch by a watchmaker and the world by God. Using this argument he concludes that an intelligent God exists, and that this God created the universe and natural world.

Paley's *a posteriori* analogy and argument – based upon experience not logic – hinges upon the assumed premise that 'like causes resemble like effects'; in this case, since machines (like the watch) and the natural world have similar features of design, both must have an intelligent designer. But Paley does not develop this assumption to tackle the question: How similar is the creation of the natural world to the creation of a watch?

One counter argument, often mistakenly attributed to David Hume (who died a quarter of a century before Paley's *Natural Theology* was published), takes the notion of 'like causes' and points out some potential flaws. One example is that a complex machine such as a watch is usually designed by a whole team of people rather than just one person, i.e. the miners and steelworkers who extract and form the materials, the factory workers who make the parts and assemble the watch, etc. Therefore, if the analogy is extended it would suggest that the natural world/universe is the work of a whole group of intelligent designers/gods and not a single, ultimate being – an argument very much at odds with Paley's monotheism.

A further objection to the analogy is that complex machines are created from a process of trial and error, with every new version undergoing a process of evolution and improvement over a number of years, the rapid developments in modern technology being an apposite example of this process. For Paley's analogy to work, then God's (or the gods') 'design' for the natural world/universe must also be an ongoing series of experiments, with flaws and imperfections that need to be ironed out and improved. But this view of God the experimenter contradicts the idea of the omnipotent and omnibenevolent ultimate being.

The principle objection to Paley's watchmaker analogy came in 1859, when Charles Darwin (1809–82) published *On the Origin of Species*. Darwin's significant and controversial work was important for many reasons, but here we need to stress:

- It introduced the scientific theory that populations evolve over the course of generations through a process of natural selection, and that the diversity of life in nature arose by common descent through a branching pattern of evolution.

- Although the first edition of Darwin's work contains several references to 'creation' and 'The Creator' – Darwin appears to believe God created species through 'the design of natural selection' – ideas about the transmutation of species were controversial as they conflicted with the beliefs that species were unchanging parts of a designed hierarchy, and that humans were unique and unrelated to other animals.

- That Darwin later changed his mind, describing his religious views as agnostic. As he wrote in his autobiography, 'the old argument of design in nature, as given by Paley, which formerly seemed to me so conclusive, fails, now that the law of natural selection has been discovered. We can no longer argue that, for instance, the beautiful hinge of a bivalve shell must have been made by an intelligent being, like the hinge of a door by man. There seems to be no more design in the variability of organic beings and in the action of natural selection, than in the course which the wind blows. Everything in nature is the result of fixed laws.'

Further objections to Paley's watchmaker analogy form the basis of evolutionary biologist Richard Dawkins' book *The Blind Watchmaker* (1986). Dawkins (b. 1941), a committed Darwinian scientist, argues that natural selection is sufficient to explain the apparent functionality and non-random complexity of the natural world, and can be said to play the role of Paley's 'watchmaker' in nature, albeit as an automatic, unguided-by-any-designer, non-intelligent, blind watchmaker of process.

THE EXISTENCE OF GOD PART 3

The problem of evil and suffering

This problem is considered to be one of the most powerful arguments against the existence of God. Put simply, how to reconcile the traditional notions of God's omnipotence and omnibenevolence with the existence of evil and suffering. The German mathematician and philosopher Gottfried Leibniz (1646–1716) developed the term 'theodicy', in his 1710 work *Theodicee*, to describe a framework that demonstrates God's existence is still plausible, despite evil and suffering. Leibniz's argument runs like this:

- He starts by affirming that God has unlimited wisdom and power and is the source of all good. However, humans are not all-powerful and are limited in their wisdom and in their power to act.

- Furthermore, God provided humans with a capacity for free will and it is precisely this capability that inclines humans to false beliefs, bad decisions and negative actions.

- God does not indiscriminately inflict pain and suffering on the world; God permits both 'moral evil' (the sinful thoughts and actions of humans) and 'physical or natural evil' (pain and suffering through natural causes beyond human control, e.g. disasters such as earthquakes, famine, disease and drought) as these are the basic consequences of 'metaphysical evil'.

- This concept of metaphysical evil describes the finite nature of life, with its limitations and imperfections, in contrast to the all-powerful perfection of God. Therefore, because humans are imperfect, forms of evil exist as a means by which humans can identify, measure and correct their flawed actions and decisions against a standard of the complete goodness possessed by God alone. But note that his concept has been criticized in scholastic (religious) philosophical circles as an incorrect concept of evil as it implies that limitations and imperfections are wrong, and there is something implicitly evil about chance and circumstance.

In 1955, the Australian philosopher J.L Mackie (1917–81) published his famous essay *Evil and Omnipotence.* He argued that the logical problem of evil arises because monotheistic religions maintain that there are no limits to God's omnipotence as he is all-powerful. Moreover, the 'theodicies' actually limit God's power but deceptively retain a conviction to the concept of 'omnipotence'. God is bound by logical necessities but permits 'natural evil' (earthquakes, etc.) as a consequence of the metaphysical evil of imperfection.

God is therefore not omnipotent as he cannot perform acts that are logically impossible because he is subject to the causal laws that he created. Nor can God turn back time to stop the conditions that caused the earthquake as this would deny the metaphysical imperfections imposed by introducing evil as a means to measure good. Therefore, God has created something he can't control and isn't omnipotent.

Many theodicies use the defence that good cannot exist without evil as evil is a necessary counterpoint against which to measure good. Mackie argues that:

- Something does not necessarily need a counterpart in order to exist. As an example, he claims that while it may be logical for other colours to exist in the universe in order for us to perceive the colour red, it is not necessarily the case. Everything in the universe could be red and although we would not have the capacity to perceive a distinction with other colours, nor would we have a name ('red') for that all-pervading colour. It would, nevertheless, still exist.

- Evil does not exist to enrich a higher level of good. For him, this argument is contradicted by the counterpoint premise – if there is a higher level of good there must in turn also be a higher level of evil over which an omnipotent God has no control. Mackie concludes that the reliance on omnipotence in theodicies is logically incompatible with the existence of evil in any form.

The American philosopher and theologian William Rowe (1931–2015), in *The Problem of Evil and Some Varieties of Atheism* (1979), proposed that while on the surface it is reasonable for God to allow some 'limited' suffering to enable humans to grow and develop ('the greater good'), it was impermissible for God to allow what Rowe termed 'intense suffering', such as the pointless suffering of defenceless animals. He used the example of a fawn caught in a forest fire as an example of pointless animal suffering.

For Rowe, an omnipotent and omniscient being would, by definition, be aware that intense suffering was occurring and could prevent the suffering from taking place. If evil and suffering was pointless, served no purpose and was avoidable, an all-loving being would probably prevent its occurrence, unless to do so would interfere with 'the greater good' or result in something equally evil and bad. As pointless and avoidable suffering is prevalent in the world, Rowe concluded that an omnipotent God does not exist. Rowe's viewpoint is known as an example of 'the evidential argument from evil'.

AUGUSTINE OF HIPPO: FROM SINNER TO SAINT

Leibniz's formulations of the 'theodicy' were heavily influenced by the ideas of the early Christian philosopher and theologian St Augustine (354–430). Born in the Roman city of Thagaste, Algeria, Augustine of Hippo studied Latin and rhetoric at Carthage, a place of renowned learning. Although born to a Christian mother and pagan father, Augustine followed the Manichean religion – a cosmological faith concerned with the eternal battle between the oppositions of good/evil and light/darkness, etc. While in Carthage, however, he was tempted into what was considered a life of sinfulness, drinking heavily and indulging his voracious sexual appetite, giving him an illegitimate child with a concubine.

Apparently one day, in a moment of reflective despair at his hedonism, Augustine ventured into a garden where he heard a child's voice telling him to go home and read. He returned to his house and the first book he opened was the Bible. Opening it at a random page, he read Paul's Epistle to the Romans (chapter 13, verses 13 and 14):

'Not in rioting and drunkenness, not in chambering and wantonness, not in strife and envying, but put on the Lord Jesus Christ, and make no provision for the flesh to fulfil the lusts thereof.' Augustine took this incident as a plea from the almighty to reject his life of excess and devote his life to God. He promptly converted to Christianity and returned to his native Algeria where he was appointed Bishop of Hippo in 396 AD.

His theodicy centres on the following:

- The argument that God created humans and angels as rational beings possessing free will.

- That it was not God's intention for free will to present a choice between good and evil – a free will in this sense is a will free from sin.

- That the fall in the Garden of Evil, caused by the disobedience of Adam and Eve, corrupted the will of human beings and bought suffering into the world.

- And while Augustine argued that free will can be corrupted, he nonetheless maintained that the existence of free will was vital in order for the human soul to embrace grace and be saved from damnation.

- In a forerunner to Leibniz's concept of metaphysical evil, Augustine also argued that evil could be exercised by humans, not because they were evil in themselves but because they didn't have the divine perfection of God, and so were corruptible although they could be saved.

Augustine devoted the rest of his life to Christianity, forsook all his worldly and material wealth, spent his time preaching and writing prodigiously and developing some of the grounding tenets of Catholic theology. St Augustine was also vehemently opposed to the practice of slavery, which he viewed as a product of sin and contrary to God's wishes. In his book *The City of God*, Augustine writes that God 'did not intend that this rational creature, who was made in his image, should have dominion over anything but the irrational creation – not man over man, but man over the beasts'.

6

What you need to know about

THE PHILOSOPHY OF LANGUAGE

The philosophy of language, particularly in the middle to late twentieth century, developed into one of the principle concerns of philosophy and related disciplines such as critical theory, social sciences and the humanities. Philosophy has a long tradition of analyzing and evaluating the functions of language, its origins, the nature of meaning, the usage and cognition of language and, in particular, relationships between language and reality.

The philosophy of language poses questions such as:

- What is meaning?
- How does language refer to the real world?

- Is language learned or is it innate?
- How does the meaning of a sentence emerge out of its parts?

PLATO AND THE NAMING OF THINGS

Plato was particularly interested in how or why we have names for things and the criteria that determines the correct choice of name for any given object. These interests are addressed in the dialogue *Cratylus,* in which Socrates is asked to settle an argument between two Athenian philosophers: the eponymous *Cratylus* and his friend Hermogenes.

Their dispute stems from a disagreement on the nature of names for objects. Cratylus formulated a thesis that the names of things are naturally derived appellations that represent objects, basic ideas, concepts or sentiments. But Hermogenes argued that names are applied to things through convention, which is in turn agreed through a consensus of the community or social grouping in which those names are used. Socrates questions Hermogenes, who concedes that an individual could apply different names for things beyond accepted communal convention and, by example, asks what is there to stop a person calling a man a horse, or vice versa. Throughout the dialogue, which contains some often unfathomable and faintly ridiculous musings on the etymology of words in the Greek language, the argument switches between Cratylus' assertion that names occur naturally as part of the essence of that which they describe ('naturalism') and Hermogenes' insistence that names are the product of convention ('conventionalism').

Socrates' position (and therefore Plato's) also seems to sway between the two diametrically opposed arguments. For example, he:

- Initially appears to be siding with Cratylus and criticizes conventionalism, perhaps in part because Cratylus' thesis echoes and corresponds with Ancient Greek metaphysics on the natural order of things in the universe.

- Argues that certain 'value words' or philosophically important concepts could not have their names arbitrarily attached to them through convention but are encoded descriptions of what they represent.

- Also argues, towards the end of the dialogue, that things could have an objective reality above and beyond what we can perceive, and so mere words cannot be regarded as perfect encapsulations of their objects' natural essence if they have a reality we cannot observe. In this sense, some element of convention needs to be adhered to and it is found in the phoneme that corresponds to the object it is describing.

ARISTOTLE ON INTERPRETATION

Plato's student Aristotle addressed one of the key questions of how meaning is conveyed through language by linking language with logic, in a systematic and formal analysis.

Aristotle's work *De Interpretatione* (*On Interpretation*) starts by defining words as 'affections of the soul'. Most scholars concur that by 'affections' (often also translated as 'passions') Aristotle is referring to functions, and by 'soul' he is referring to the human mind. Therefore, affections/passions of the soul are workings of the mind or, specifically, mechanisms through which the mind orders and perceives things, of which words are a key component.

Aristotle begins *De Interpretatione* by:

- Setting out categories and their distinct functions, similarities and contradictions.

- He then asserts that although spoken and written symbols differ between languages, the mental experiences are the same for all. For example, the

English word 'cat' and the Spanish '*gato*' are different symbols, but the mental experience they stand for – the concept of a cat – is the same for English and Spanish speakers.

- And, furthermore, says that nouns and verbs in isolation cannot determine truth or falsity. In contrast to Plato, Aristotle argues that nouns (names) provide significance to the subject they describe by convention but have no reference to time, though verbs are, when structured into tenses, reflective of time. For example: 'I will eat fish tonight' (future time) and by contrast, 'I ate fish yesterday' (past time). Verbs in isolation can only relate to present time.

- Aristotle then turns his attention to sentences and argues that although words in isolation have significance, only sentences (words in relation to each other) have the capacity to form coherent expressions such as questions, statements and exclamations. Sentences, through the inter relations of their constituent parts (subject and predicate), are able to affirm or negate expressions.

- This distinction between how meaning is conveyed differently by words in isolation and words in combination is important to Aristotle, as in relation to philosophy it has profound implications for evaluating propositions.

- Simple propositions contain a verb, which modifies the subject of the sentence and indicate a single fact ('It will rain today'). Complex propositions consist of several propositions in compound form: 'The wind will move the clouds and it won't rain today.'

- We affirm or deny the validity of propositions by making assertions. For example, 'humans are animals' asserts that humans belong to the animal kingdom. Conversely 'trees are not animals' denies that 'trees' are 'animals'.

- Aristotle then expands his analysis towards what he describes as 'universal propositions' and the problem of contradictions. Of contradictions, one must be true, the other false. Contraries cannot both be true, although they can both be false, and hence their contradictories are both true. For example, 'Every politician is a liar' and 'No politician is a liar' are both false. But their contradictories, 'some politicians tell the truth' and 'some politicians do not tell the truth', are both deemed to be true.

- When analyzing contradictory propositions in relation to the past and present, one must be true, the other false. So, 'it rained yesterday' and 'it didn't rain yesterday' provide binary oppositions (it either rained or it didn't). However, when the subject is expressed in a future proposition the true/false rule does not apply, as this would negate elements of chance.

The problem of future contingents

Aristotle framed the problem of chance in future propositions with what is known as the 'sea battle example'. Take the proposition 'a sea battle will take place' and its contrary, 'a sea battle will not take place'. In both, one will either be true or false to correspond with future reality. However, if there is a sea battle then it was always true that there would be a sea battle as what is true in the future is also true in the past. Conversely, if there is not a sea battle then it was also always true that there would not be a sea battle.

But this future event/past truth dichotomy throws up the following problem: if it was always true that there would be a sea battle then there was never a point when anybody could prevent it, and to the contrary, if always true that there wouldn't be a sea battle, there was never a point where anyone could have instigated it. Thus, either the occurrence of the sea battle is necessary, or the nonoccurrence of the sea battle is necessary. And the 'necessity' that this argument attaches to events is necessity of the past. So, we are to think of our powerlessness to affect the constitution of the future as we conceive of our inability to affect the constitution of the past. Just as the past is now closed to us, so too is our future.

Aristotle's fundamental solution was to deny that future contingent statements had truth values, and so 'there will be a sea battle' and 'there will not be a sea battle' were both neither true nor false:

> One of the two propositions in such instances must be true and the other false, but we cannot say determinately that this or that is false, but must leave the alternative undecided. One may indeed be more likely to be true than the other, but it cannot be either actually true or actually false. It is therefore plain that it is not necessary that of an affirmation and a denial, one should be true and the other false. For in the case of that which exists potentially, but not actually, the rule which applies to that which exists actually does not hold good.
>
> ARISTOTLE *ON INTERPRETATION*
>
> (TRANS. E.M. EDGHILL)

WHAT IS MEANING?

Interest in the philosophy of language underwent something of a renaissance in the nineteenth and twentieth centuries, particularly through the pioneering work of Gottlob Frege (1848–1925), Ludwig Wittgenstein and Bertrand Russell (1872–1970), and after the publication of *Cours de linguistique générale* (*Course in general linguistics*) by Ferdinand de Saussure (1857–1913), which was published posthumously in 1916.

Saussure's thesis proved to be highly influential and paved the way for the development of semiotics (the science of signs and symbols) and structuralism (a theoretical framework for uncovering underlying patterns in human thought and behaviour). In regard to Saussure's contribution to linguistics, the foundation was the theory that language is comprised of two separate levels, which he defined as '*langue*' and '*parole*'.

- The level of '*langue*' involves the underlying principles and systematic rules, abstractions and conventions that comprise a language (Saussure used the term 'signifying system' as *langue* can refer to visual or non-verbal languages).

- '*Parole*' (which means 'speaking') is the act of communicating, either verbally or through writing or via signs and gestures. It is by understanding the relationship of the two parts of a sign through *langue* that the essence of communication or *parole* may be understood.

Devoid of the understanding of *langue*, *parole* would be meaningless sounds or symbols assembled arbitrarily. Saussure used the game of chess as an analogy to explain how *langue* and *parole* work together. *Langue* corresponds to the rules of a chess game while *parole* is represented by the individual players' choice of moves. It is possible to analyze all of the individual moves in a game of chess (the *parole*) and derive from this analysis (through identifying repeated patterns) the rules that govern the game, but in effect all this process would entail is the unmasking of the *langue* – the governing principles that make the game function as a cohesive whole.

Although Saussure's ideas provide a theoretical framework for the structure of meaning in communication, they fall short of addressing how meaning relates to and represents the world around us. Frege proposed that to establish and understand how language represents reality, a distinction is required within our intuitive notion of meaning, roughly corresponding to Saussure's *langue*.

Frege was an early advocate of what is known in linguistics as a mediated reference theory, but what does it involve?

- That words or signs refer to something in the external world, and that there is more to the meaning of a sign than simply the object (or thing) to which it relates.

- Frege made this distinction by dividing the semantic value of every expression (including sentences) into two components, which he named *Sinn* (roughly translates as 'sense') and *Bedeutung* ('meaning' or 'reference').

- The *Sinn* of a sentence is the abstract, universal and objective thought that it expresses, but also the mode of presentation of the object that it refers to.

- The *Bedeutung* is the object or objects in the real world that words relate to, in as much as they represent a truth-value (true or the false).

- Sense determines reference, but names that refer to the same object can have different senses.

Noam Chomsky's language revolution

In the mid-1950s, the American linguist and philosopher Professor Noam Chomsky (b. 1928) started a revolution in linguistic analysis and in his *Synthetic Structures* (1957). He challenged the accepted view that children acquire language through instruction and experience. For him, the speed with which language is mastered suggested that there must be an innate predisposition for language. He took this to mean that an unlearned universal grammar exists, supplying rules that can be recognized immediately, whatever the language encountered, and that there are two levels of linguistic knowledge: deep structures, which refer to the universal grammar shared by all languages, and surface structures, which cover specific sounds and words used in a particular language. Chomsky believes that we are all hard-wired for language, and he reiterated the rationalist and empiricist implications of this idea in *Cortesian Linguistics* (1966).

- Frege illustrates his argument with reference to two expressions commonly used to describe the planet Venus: 'the morning star' and 'the evening star'. Although both expressions share the same reference (*Bedeutung*), the sense (*Sinn*) is different in reality as Venus can be visible at different times of day.

The answer to the question 'What is meaning?' is more complex than it appears. A dictionary definition describes meaning as the content carried by the words or signs (or actions) exchanged by people when communicating, either intentionally or unintentionally through a form of language. It could be argued that there are two essentially distinct forms of linguistic meaning. First, conceptual meanings that refer to the definitions of words themselves and the aspects of those definitions, including their individual semantic value. Second, the associative meanings, which refer to the individual mental identifications of the person communicating, and these may be reflective and/or determined by collective and social connotation.

WITTGENSTEIN AND THE USE THEORY OF LANGUAGE

Ludwig Wittgenstein was one of the most important philosophers of the twentieth century and published two books devoted to the philosophy of language: *Tractatus Logico Philosophicus* (1921) and the *Philosophical Investigations* (1953). The remarkable aspect of Wittgenstein's writing on language is that his position differs quite radically between the two works. The *Tractatus* (which became his doctoral thesis at Cambridge University) outlines the basis for a representational theory of language, which he termed 'picture theory'.

For Wittgenstein, at least in his early work, what we understand as the 'reality' of the 'world' is an immense assortment of propositions. The purpose of propositions is to establish facts (true or false) and primarily facts that can be viewed or 'pictured' in language. 'The world is the totality of facts, not of things', he argued, and our comprehension of these facts is necessarily ordered by logic. The purpose of philosophy, therefore, is to strip language back to its logical forms in order that we can have a clearer picture of the reality of the world. The issue of course is that language that does not deal with these picture/facts – speculations, feelings, aesthetic descriptions, value judgements, etc. – and does not comply with pure logic and is thus rendered meaningless. Hence Wittgenstein's famous dictum at the close of the *Tractatus*: 'That whereof we cannot speak, thereof we must remain silent' or, put another way, language and by extension human thought are limited in relation to reality of the world as it really is.

The *Tractatus* proved to be a big influence upon a group of academics centred around Vienna University between the two world wars. The logical positivists, as they became known, set about debunking what they deemed as 'unverifiable' propositions through applying logic to philosophical problems. Wittgenstein, however, was not a member of this group having decided he'd said all he could about philosophy, or hadn't said what he couldn't say, and he abandoned the discipline and became a school teacher, a gardener and retrained as an architect, designing and building a house in Vienna for his sister Gretl.

One of the key points about Wittgenstein is that his second work, *Philosophical Investigations,* tracks the shift in his thinking during his second period at Cambridge. The change is from viewing language as a fixed structure imposed upon the world to seeing it as fluid and closely bound up with our everyday practices and forms of social life. The meaning in language, Wittgenstein argued, was not, as he had previously asserted, a process of mapping the logical form of the world as it is. Meaning in language is derived from conventionally defined terms that form

Wittgenstein: how to win friends and influence people

At the suggestion of his friend and mentor Bertrand Russell (and in order to secure a teaching and research position at Cambridge), Wittgenstein was encouraged to submit the manuscript of *Tractus Logico Philosophicus* to obtain his PhD. The panel for the *viva voce* (oral examination) consisted of Russell, G.E. Moore (1873–1958) and Norman Malcolm (1911–90), three of the most notable intellectuals in the UK. Wittgenstein is alleged to have started the meeting by slamming his thesis down on the desk and saying 'We can talk about this all day and you three will still never understand it.' Moore remarked later that there were large parts of the *Tractus* that he found difficult to grasp but it was well above the standard of most doctoral presentations, so he agreed to his doctorate.

'language games', played out in our everyday existence. 'In most cases, the meaning of a word is its use,' he wrote, asserting that meaning derives not from the meaning of the words in and of themselves, but the manner in which they are expressed and the contexts in which they are deployed. This model for communication relies upon the use of conventionally recognized terms and signs specific to a particular linguistic community.

Communication, on this model, involves using conventional terms in a way that is recognized by a linguistic community and playing a conventionally accepted 'language game'. Wittgenstein's theories also give space to non-verbal language, gesture, movement and body language and argue that the reason, for example, humans cannot directly communicate with most animals is because we do not understand their language games any more than they can understand ours.

To further expand upon the use value of language, Wittgenstein draws a distinction between public and private language. The historic distinction between the two is that public language relates to the language used in discourse (communication) and private language to the language of the mind (our inner thoughts). It was Wittgenstein's conviction that all language is socially acquired and so therefore that all language is a public language of one form or another, and that private language therefore doesn't exist in isolation from a certain context. Wittgenstein uses the metaphor of an idle wheel to debunk the view that the private language of the mind can exist independently: 'A wheel that can be turned but nothing else moves with it.'

The eccentric Wittgenstein

During his time at Cambridge, Wittgenstein was renowned as much for his intellectual brilliance as his often highly eccentric behaviour. A former colleague and close friend, the mathematician and philosopher Norman Malcolm, describes in vivid detail Wittgenstein's bizarre antics in his memoirs. Here are just three examples:

- One infamous anecdote, often disputed by his followers, claims that he once threatened the esteemed philosopher Karl Popper with a red-hot poker during a meeting of the Cambridge University Moral Science Club.

- Wittgenstein's lectures, which Malcolm often attended, would begin with a simple premise – usually something that Wittgenstein disagreed with – and spiral into multiple digressions until he found something more interesting to talk about. From time to time Wittgenstein would suddenly stop speaking and stare at the students, as if waiting for one of them to ask a question. Silence would prevail, often for up to twenty minutes, before Wittgenstein would commence speaking again.

Why can't dogs simulate pain?

When the rigour of his intellectual pursuits began to make him weary, Wittgenstein's main method of relaxation – other than watching B-movie Westerns at the local cinema – was to go for long walks along the riverbank. Malcolm noticed that when Wittgenstein, noted for his fiery temperament and intensity, was at one with natural surroundings, he would relax and tell jokes, usually on a philosophical theme.

On one occasion, out of nothing, Wittgenstein suddenly turned to Malcolm and asked, 'Why can't dogs simulate pain? Do you think it's because they are too honest?' Wittgenstein's sly joke is not a proposition or an empirical truth about dogs and their honesty or innate psychology, proven or otherwise. It is a language game around human understanding about concepts attached to the words 'dog', 'pain', 'simulate' and 'honest'. Wittgenstein deliberately places the words into an absurd context in order to question their value.

- At the outbreak of the Second World War, Wittgenstein, who had only recently been elected as a full professor of philosophy, was so incensed by the conflict that he took a job as a porter at Guy's Hospital during the blitz. One of his duties was to tour the wards dispensing drugs. In true Wittgenstein fashion, he would often engage his patients in philosophical arguments on the nature of pain and suffering and discourage them from taking medicine.

BERTRAND RUSSELL: LOGICAL ATOMISM AND THE THEORY OF DESCRIPTIONS

Wittgenstein's ideas about language, particularly as outlined in *Tractatus Logico Philosophicus,* found much favour with his mentor and friend Bertrand Russell's theory of logical atomism. Russell's philosophical method contended that, via rigorous and challenging analysis, language could be broken down into component parts. Once a sentence cannot be dismantled any further, all that remains are its 'logical atoms'. It is then by thorough examination of the atoms that comprise statements and propositions that underlying assumptions can be exposed and their truth or validity properly assessed.

In his essay *On Denoting* (1905), Russell uses the following statement to illustrate his theory: 'The present King of France is bald.' Russell then breaks down this seemingly straightforward statement into its logical atoms:

- There is a present King of France.
- There is only one present King of France.
- The present King of France no longer has any hair on his head.

Russell knew that France abolished their monarchy in 1792 and, despite some periods of restoration, France has essentially been a republic since 1870. So the first assumption can be deemed false as there was then no 'present King of France'; and therefore the second assumption is also false. However, taken in its entirety, the complete statement 'The present King of France is bald' although untrue, cannot be deemed to be completely *false* in the classical sense because the opposite ('The present King of France has hair') is equally untrue. This is because the contrary persists with the assumption that there is a 'present King of France' when there isn't.

So, the philosophical problem is this. If the sentence is neither true nor false, does it in fact contain any meaning at all? Russell, through his application of logical atomism, is posing a further, more profound question: How is it possible to meaningfully describe things that don't exist when traditional concepts of truth and validity are underpinned by complex and ambiguous assumptions?

It was Russell's belief that common, everyday usage of language, given its capacity to be misleading and riddled with vagaries, was not able to accurately represent truth. A fundamental issue in philosophical inquiry therefore is to rid itself of errors and assumptions, and develop a pure, formal methodology based on the rigours of mathematical logic. To this end, Russell's theory proposed a process for understanding statements by identifying definite descriptions.

A definite description is defined as words, names or phrases that denote specific, individual objects or entities such as 'table', 'Adolf Hitler' and 'America'. Russell argued that the meaning (or semantic value) of names is identical to the descriptions associated with them by speakers, but contextually appropriate descriptions can be substituted for the name. However, Russell asserted that only directly referential expressions are what he called 'logically proper names' such as, 'I', 'now' and 'here'. Russell termed proper nouns of people or objects, e.g. 'London', 'David' or 'Helicopter', as 'abbreviated definite descriptions' with the name acting as a substitute for a more detailed description of who or what the person, place or object actually is. 'Abbreviated definite descriptions', however, are not meaningful in isolation as they cannot be considered directly referential.

Russell devised his theory of descriptions as a means to address problems posed by sentences such as 'The present King of France is bald'; propositions where the object to which the definite description refers is ambiguous or non-existent, and he termed such expressions 'incomplete symbols'. By illustrating how they can be dismantled into their logical atoms, Russell's method aimed to reveal how the truth and validity of certain statements can be obscured by grammatical form. Russell's project was to provide a tool-kit that could enable philosophers and linguists to uncover the logical structures hidden in everyday language in order to avoid ambiguity and paradox when constructing arguments and propositions.

JACQUES DERRIDA: WHAT NO MEANING?

The French philosopher Jacques Derrida (1930–2004) was born into a Sephardic family (an ethnic Jewish group particular to Spain and Portugal) in the city of El Biar, in French Algeria. Derrida's early education was disrupted by the dictates of the Vichy government, which banned Jewish children from formal state education. At the age of ten, after being told by one of his teachers that 'French culture is not made for little Jews', Derrida was expelled and sent to the local, separate Jewish school. However, he rarely attended classes and spent most of his time reading and playing football, and indeed harboured ambitions to be a professional footballer. During this period he developed a passion for the philosophy of Rousseau and Nietzsche and, at the age of nineteen, went to Paris to study philosophy at the prestigious *École Normale Superieure*, gaining his master's degree in 1954. He taught philosophy at a number of prominent universities around the world, including the Sorbonne in Paris, and Yale and John Hopkins universities in the US, and published three groundbreaking books in 1967: *Writing and Difference*, *Speech and Phenomena* and *Of Grammatology*. These formed the bedrock of Derrida's philosophy of language and outlined his analytical method of 'deconstruction'.

Derrida's main theory was a wholesale rejection of the structuralist view of language, created by Saussure:

- His view was centred on the human tendency to think in terms of oppositions.

- For Saussure, the binary opposition was the 'means by which the units of language have value or meaning; each unit is defined against what it is not.'

With this categorization, terms and concepts tend to be associated with a positive or negative. Such pairings include Reason and Passion, Man and Woman, Inside and Outside, Presence and Absence, Speech and Writing, etc.

- But Derrida argued that these oppositions were arbitrary and inherently unstable. Or put another way, why is one part of the opposition positive and the other negative and not the other way around?

- Furthermore, he believed that by 'deconstructing' these oppositions, the structures themselves start to merge, overlap and conflict, and dismantle themselves from within the text.

So deconstruction rejects binary opposition on the grounds that such oppositions always privilege one term over the other. In Saussurean terms, the 'signified' (the meaning) holds sway over the 'signifier' (the sign or symbol). In Derrida's deconstruction, the separation between symbol and meaning becomes blurred.

Derrida uses the term 'logocentrism' to describe what he sees as the widely held flaw in western philosophy, that speech and not writing is central to language. Logocentrism proposes that:

- Speech is the original signifier (sign) of meaning, and the written word is derived from the spoken word.

- The written word is thus a representation of the spoken word.

- Language originates as a process of thought which, in turn, produces speech, and that speech then yields writing.

- Logocentrism itself is that nature of texts, ideas, modes of representation and signifying systems that creates a need for a direct grip on meaning, existence and understanding.

Derrida's deconstruction is a strategy of critical questioning directed towards exposing the seemingly incontestable, metaphysical assumptions and internal contradictions characteristic of philosophical and literary language. The method concerns a 'practice' of reading texts by 'decentering' or looking as much for what is absent or unspoken as for what is apparent and innate. By rejecting concepts such as 'analysis' and 'interpretation', deconstruction aims to unmask the inherent instability of meaning in language and the assumptions behind how language functions in discourse.

7

What you need to know about

THE PHILOSOPHY OF LOVE

The philosophy of love is an area of social philosophy that examines the concept of love in its different forms and how it impacts upon human relationships. Philosophically, the nature of love has, since the time of the Ancient Greeks, been a mainstay of philosophical enquiry and has produced various theories that range from a materialistic conception of love closely related to physical desires and genetic urgings, to spiritual notions of love as a deep connection between individuals that fosters virtue, friendship and happiness. In theology, a distinction is often made between earthly love that exists between people (and people and objects) and other-worldly love, i.e. transcendent, unconditional and reciprocal love of God for man and man for God. The philosophy of love asks questions such as:

- What is love?
- What is the relationship between the lover and the beloved? How does love relate to duty and responsibility?

SOCRATES: DIOTIMA'S 'LADDER OF LOVE'

In Plato's *The Symposium*, Socrates outlines a view of love by arguing that, if love is material, then it consists of something, and if of something then it is an object that is desired, hence something to be possessed. Socrates then recounts a dialogue with the High Priestess Diotima of Mantinea, whom he claims is an expert on matters of love.

Diotima (whose name means 'honoured by the God, Zeus') states that love, in the first form, consists of the desire of beautiful and exceptionally good things, and particularly of wisdom, which is both beautiful and good. Diotima adds that love must not be confused with the object of love, which, in contrast to Eros (love itself, and the god of sensual love and desire), is perfectly beautiful and perfectly good. The Greeks believed that Eros was the spirit-driving human love, and yet although this is a starting point, this is not love, but a shallow desire to possess the object of affection. In a famous section, Diotima states that love in this sense is not a god, but Eros is 'in truth the child of poverty and resource, always in need, but always inventive'.

Diotima then instructs Socrates in how to ascend the *scala amoris* (ladder of love):

- The first step is to acknowledge and desire a beautiful, perfect youth.

- Next, move from loving one individual body to recognizing the qualities it shares with other beautiful bodies, and thus that it is folly to love just one beautiful body. This realization leads to the next rung of the ladder.

- By appreciating the beauty of all, one learns to appreciate that the beauty of the soul is greater than the beauty of the body, and in turn learns to love those who are beautiful in soul regardless of whether they are also beautiful in body.

- The realization that one has transcended the physical realm of love leads to an understanding of the beauty that resides in other areas, and that practices and customs and the various forms of knowledge also share in a common beauty. The mastering of this next rung on the ladder allows the individual to comprehend and experience beauty in and of itself, rather than the various superficial versions of beauty.

- Put simply, Diotima's ladder of love is a journey of self-realization, which involves transcending and exchanging the various apparitions of virtue of beauty for virtue itself. It is suggested that the ultimate destination in this journey of love and life is to reach an immortality of the soul and the reverence of the gods.

In his *Nicomachean Ethics* (*c.* 350 BC) Aristotle introduces a concept of love centred around virtues of friendship and loyalty which he terms '*philia*'. For Aristotle the pursuit of *Eudaimonia* (happiness or a happy or fulfilling life) involves the exercise of reason because the capacity to reason is the distinctive function of human beings. Nonetheless, it could be argued that another distinctive purpose of human beings is not only the capacity to reason but also the capacity to form meaningful, loving relationships.

Aristotle viewed *philia* as directing love towards families, friends and communities through the exercise of virtues such as equality, generosity of spirit and simple kindness. Aristotle also argues that *philia* can also be exercised in an abstract and emotive sense to describe how love can be explored through experience and feelings stirred by the beauty of art, poetry and music, or the love of nature. Plato reconciles these positions by merging desire (eros), friendship (*philia*) and philosophy (the love of wisdom) into a single, total experience that transcends and transforms human existence, and connects it with the timeless and universal truths of the eternal and infinite (the Greek concept of *agape* or other-worldly love). For Plato, truth and authenticity are of a higher value than either reason or love, which aim at them, and of a higher value even than happiness, which is merely the manifestation of their presence.

What is platonic love?

As most people know, a platonic relationship is one that is affectionate, intimate even, but stops short of being sexual. What not many people know is that this definition harks back to Plato and his doctrine of 'forms'. Plato alleges that beyond the sexual desire that is constantly coursing through the material world, demanding immediate satisfaction, lies the idealized form of beauty that true love aspires to: platonic love.

JEAN-PAUL SARTRE: LOVE AS STRUGGLE AND CONFLICT

Sartre (1905–80) was a major proponent of the philosophical doctrine of existentialism outlined in his numerous literary works that included critical essays, novels and plays. Central to his thinking is the view that people have no essential 'essence' – human beings are born and exist, but as God does not exist there is no essence to human life; 'existence precedes essence'. In his celebrated essay *Existentialism and Humanism* (1946), Sartre writes: 'What do we mean by saying that existence precedes essence? We mean that man first of all exists, encounters himself, surges up in the world and defines himself. If man as the existentialist sees him is not definable it is because to begin with he is nothing.'

Sartre argues that:

- When humans analyze their own being, what they discover at the centre of it is *nothing*.
- However, this 'nothingness' is simultaneously a blessing and a curse.
- On one hand, humans are totally free to create their own 'self' and live the life they desire. On the other,

this freedom comes at a price or in a negative sense precisely because there is nothing to constrain us from being free.

So, in his book *Being and Nothingness* (1943), Sartre asserts that 'Man, being condemned to be free carries the whole weight of the world on his shoulders; he is responsible for the world and for himself as a way of being.' Although we are each individually conscious beings, we require the acknowledgement of others to validate our essence and 'make us real'. In short, to create our own self and feel complete, we must join our 'nothingness' to another's 'being'.

In terms of human relationships, Sartre poses the problem of how individuals reconcile their freedom to self-determination with the need to be wanted by 'another' in order to validate our being. Here's the argument:

- In terms of love, the individual seeking love wishes to be loved by someone who has freely chosen to love them.

- Sartre uses the legend of Tristan and Isolde, who gain eternal love by accidentally drinking a love potion, as an example of false love because they have not consciously or freely joined with each other.

- However, the problem lies in attempting to turn the free consciousness of other people into objects, which is impossible. We cannot possess people in the same way that we can possess an object, because objects cannot reciprocate that possession. People can try to make others dependent emotionally, or materially, but can never possess the consciousness of another.

- Humanity's best chance for happiness or success in relationships is to recognize and allow another's freedom, despite the natural wish to 'own' them.

In attempting to possess a person as an object, humans necessarily endeavour to possess their loved one's conscious freedom to need them: 'the Lover wants to be "the whole World" for the beloved'. The lover must become 'the ground' for the loved and represent to them the ultimate frontier of their freedom and wish for them to freely elect to perceive no further. From the lover's perspective, Sartre writes: 'I must no longer be seen on the ground of the world as a "this" among other "thises", but the world must be revealed in terms of me.'

Ironically, Sartre argues, in the desire to possess their beloved's freedom, the lover relinquishes their own freedom through the act of demanding that they are the centre of their beloved's existence. At this point the lover's actual predicament emerges because they are dependent on their beloved, and this dependency alienates them from their own essential freedom: 'It is the one who wants to be loved who by the mere fact of wanting someone to love [them] alienates [their] freedom.'

The power of romantic relationships, for Sartre, lies in the merging together of one person's state of Nothingness and another's Being. Although humans rely on confirmation from the 'other' for our 'essence' (otherwise, we are the state of Nothing), we are perpetually insecure in love because at any moment we can become, instead of the centre of the lover's world, merely one thing among many – a 'this' among 'thises'.

Love therefore becomes a matter of struggle and conflict through the inability to ever truly possess another's consciousness. Sartre argues that the lover feels the need to be loved by the object of his ardour but in doing so can turn himself from a free subject into an object, through compliance and acquiescence, and by being constrained by their beloved's expectations. This, Sartre states, is akin to a form of masochism. Alternatively, the lover can seek to control their beloved by limiting their freedom and essence and thereby subjectifying their individuality, which for Sartre amounts to a form of sadism.

It is the struggle between objectivity and subjectivity

that lies at the centre of all conflicts and unresolved issues in love. Relationships are a constant battle between lovers needing to perceive each other's freedom and desiring to possess each other as an object. Remove the other's freedom and they are no longer attractive and love is 'inauthentic'. However, if they are in not some way an object they cannot be possessed. The only answer for Sartre lies in the recognition and acceptance of the other person's freedom as this is the only way we can possibly 'possess' them.

NIETZSCHE ON LOVE AND WOMEN

Friedrich Wilhelm Nietzsche was born in Röcken, near Leipzig, Prussia. His father was a Lutheran pastor, who died suddenly of a brain tumour when Nietzsche was five years old, leaving him and his younger sister to be raised by their mother, grandmother and two unmarried aunts. Commentators have often speculated that Nietzsche's complex and often contradictory attitudes to women were influenced by this female-dominated environment of his upbringing.

In his work *Human, All Too Human* (1878), Nietzsche lays out his philosophical investigations into human life and relationships via a series of aphorisms – short,

Practise what you preach?

John Paul Sartre certainly practised what he preached when it came to relationships. After meeting the writer Simone de Beauvoir (1908–66) in 1929, the two young academics became lovers and maintained an open relationship which lasted until Sartre's death in 1980. Although one of the most famous 'literary couples' of the twentieth century, the two never married, cohabitated or had any children together. This was in part a rebellion against what they both perceived as the bourgeois values of their respective upbringings, but also a commitment to not place any false limits on their capacity for freedom and experience. Both Sartre and de Beauvoir had other lovers during their relationship, the latter most famously the American novelist Nelson Algren, whom, curiously, de Beauvoir addressed in correspondence as 'my beloved husband'. Despite living apart, the two French writers would meet up on almost a daily basis when in Paris, drink coffee, chain smoke and read and encourage each other's work, a model of recognizing each other's freedom within a relationship.

unqualified statements and observations, a style that was to become the hallmark of his writings. *Human, All Too Human* is a collection of over 680 aphorisms divided into nine, loosely themed sections covering topics ranging from metaphysics to morality to religion, and from friendship to gender studies. In his section entitled 'Women and Child' Nietzsche states: 'The perfect woman is a higher type of human than the perfect man, and also something much more rare. The natural science of animals offers a means to demonstrate the probability of this tenet.' This is a curious notion, and one which has perplexed feminist scholars, as Nietzsche appears to be arguing that by virtue of the capacity to bear children, women are a superior species.

On the psychology of women and child-rearing, Nietzsche suggests in aphorism 387 that 'Some mothers need happy, respected children; some need unhappy children: otherwise they cannot demonstrate their goodness as mothers.' In this quote Nietzsche's love of oppositions and contradictions is apparent. It would seem to be axiomatic, from a moral perspective, that all parents wish the best for their child and yearn to be proud of their achievements and happiness. However, it is in the sly use of the word 'need' in relation to motherhood that Nietzsche reveals the contradiction. Do women really seek self-validation through their child? And to need a child to be sick in order to demonstrate your goodness is akin

Nietzsche: unlucky in love?

The subject of Nietzsche's personal life has been a contentious issue among modern philosophers. Theories range from Nietzsche living a life of abject celibacy to one of rampant bisexuality. Nietzsche's descent into mental illness prior to his death was thought for many years to be the result of having contracted syphilis from regular visits to brothels in Cologne and Genoa. This theory has been largely discredited by modern commentators, preferring instead to cite Nietzsche's frequent battles with illness as more akin to symptoms of a manic depressive disorder. Nevertheless, Nietzsche became besotted with the writer, psychoanalyst and protégé of Sigmund Freud, Lou Andreas-Salomé (1861–1937), and he proposed to her on three separate occasions, only to be flatly rejected each time.

to the psychopathic disorder known as Munchausen by proxy, where parents deliberately conspire to make their child ill so they will need their care and attention.

Further contempt for what appears to be an attack on the conceit of motherhood can be found in the aphorism when Nietzsche states: 'Mothers are easily jealous of their sons' friends if they are exceptionally successful. Usually a mother loves *herself* in her son more than she loves the son himself.' It therefore becomes problematic to actually see how Nietzsche is making a coherent argument for 'the perfect woman' as a 'higher type of human', unless he is pointing out the follies that deny this perfection and make it 'much more rare'.

On the subject of relationships between men and women, Nietzsche seems to take a pragmatic approach: 'The best friend will probably get the best wife, because a good marriage is based on a talent for friendship.' For Nietzsche, friendship and the sharing of experiences supersedes the need for physical attraction or romantic infatuations. At one point he goes so far as to recommend that male/female relationships function better where physical attraction is subjugated or absent: 'Women can very well enter into a friendship with a man, but to maintain it – a little physical antipathy must help out.'

Ultimately, Nietzsche's view of marriage is that it is doomed if the romantic idyll is placed at the base: 'Marriages that are made for love (so-called love matches) have Error as their father and Necessity (need) as their mother.' This aphorism illustrates the inner contradictions and oppositions in many of Nietzsche's proclamations as, in the original German, the 'Necessity' part of the statement reads *'die Not (das Bedürfnis)'*. In German '*die Not*' can mean an urge or desire to be fulfilled while 'Not' is often used to describe a dire and miserable situation. As with much of Nietzsche's writing, literal interpretation is problematic, and in the marriage example above is Nietzsche suggesting women who marry supposedly for love are fulfilling a yearning need or entering into a miserable situation?

8

What you need to know about

THE PHILOSOPHY OF THE FUTURE

Modern philosophy in the twenty-first century can be loosely split into three domains. The first is academic philosophy. As an academic discipline, philosophy is often accused of being too self-referential. This is a shame, as a love of wisdom should be cherished and preserved along with the right to question the world around us, two things that lie at the heart of philosophy.

The second involves forms of communication and the mass media, which may generally be termed 'the philosophy of the street'. Rapid developments in information technology have opened up new areas where information can be rapidly dispersed across the globe. In a world full of unintelligible and often meaningless blurbs communicated instantly at the press of a button, there is a desperate and continuing need for careful, disciplined thinking and language. Indeed, new technologies, with their promises and threats, bring an urgency to traditional questions about liberty and the nature of the good society, concerns of philosophy since the time of the Ancient Greeks. But technological advances bring their own anxieties encumbered in the modern surveillance society of data mining, personality profiling and ubiquitous public surveillance cameras. What are the implications of these factors on notions of personal privacy and freedom?

The third and perhaps most vital area today involves the sciences and social sciences (i.e. politics and economics). Global warming presents grave dangers for the future of the human race and sustainability of the planet. This has given rise to various strands of eco-philosophy addressing pressing questions about the distribution of the world's resources, and about the nature of justice in a global society. The social science of economics, and in particular the free market's capability to create an economy suitable for the majority of people, has been questioned in the light of continuing global recession. Some contemporary economists and philosophers question whether a system that enriches a few seemingly at the expense of the many should be made subject to greater state intervention, while others have come forward to defend the system.

PHILOSOPHY AND (1) POPULISM

The recent rise of so-called 'populism' is seen by some to represent a backlash against globalization and liberal capitalism. It actually presents some interesting philosophical questions as it seems to derive its power from emotive anger, soundbites and slogans that often don't stand up to scrutiny; opinions presented as fact – a form of extreme subjectivism.

AND (2) MASS MIGRATION

Certain political theorists also question if military intervention to topple dictatorial regimes or, as they often claim, to protect precious mineral resources, is desirable and effective, as it seems to result in costly military occupations and impacts upon domestic economies and the quality of life. The humanitarian cost of such political, military and economic interventions has fed directly into mass migration – a favourite issue for many populist politicians, and one that has deep moral and ethical philosophical concerns. Likewise, the rise of militant Islam and its implications for free speech, tolerance and other liberal democratic values is also a source of ongoing contemporary philosophical debate.

AND (3) HEALTH CARE

A further issue in the philosophy of the future may concern matters relating to health care. Western democracies have seen average life expectancy rising steadily since the middle of the last century. This throws up questions of dealing with an aging population: how sustainable is current provision in terms of resources and what are the moral duties involved? Science and medicine have a role to play in ongoing debates on health. Other dilemmas concern euthanasia and the right to die, and bio-ethical issues resulting from scientific advancements in genome research and other medical developments. The possibility of creating spare organs by 'harvesting' stem-cells from cloned human foetuses that are later destroyed has been both opposed by parties stressing the 'sanctity of life', and championed by others who stress the benefits to medical science and wider society. The area of bio-ethics could become increasingly central to future philosophical debate as the capacity to successfully clone, and to manipulate the human genome, advances.

AND TO CONCLUDE ...

The philosophy of the future has many challenges to face, ranging from the impact of technology upon individuals and communities, the ecological preservation of the planet and sustainability of resources, and the instability of a globalized economy to future developments in science and medicine. Philosophy does not provide a framework for finding easy answers and solutions for the problems facing the modern world, but what it does provide are the tools with which to think and make our own judgements. It follows that if people are denied the capacity to evaluate and interpret the world there is little hope of changing it for the better of all. Change is affected as new concepts, theories and paradigms come to the fore and challenge received ideas and practices of the past.

To remain relevant in the modern age and not be consigned to a library of quaint old books about knowledge, philosophy must revive its original place in the public sphere, like the market place of Ancient Athens, where the philosophers of the day gathered to campaign, challenge and debate. There is a need to bring clarity of thinking about things that really matter and not become clouded by the blizzard of information swirling around us. Philosophy needs the confidence to be engaged in the issues of the day but it also needs dialogue; philosophy cannot take place in a vacuum.

APPENDIX

Philosophical terms

The following is a brief lexicography of philosophical terminology for really busy people. One note of caution however; although every effort has been made to provide succinct and accurate definitions of the proliferation of 'isms' and 'ologies' that comprise the study and practice of philosophy, some of the terminology is open to interpretation and discussion. This is in part because certain ideas and schools of thought were fluid and developed and refined over time, and also because some philosophical concepts, by their nature, resisted or rejected definition.

Successive thinkers in the history of philosophy have adopted ideas and taken those ideas into different directions by applying them to the world as they saw it during their epoch. Epicurus' conception of consequentialism would differ markedly from that of Jeremy Bentham and John Stuart Mill just as the prevailing culture and social norms differ from Ancient Greece and nineteenth century Europe. But I hope it provides at least a useful pointer for where to find more detailed discussion of key concepts and ideas.

Atomism: a view of the composition of the universe in which nature is constructed of 'atoms' and a 'void'. Atoms move freely through the void either attracting or repelling other atoms. Attracting atoms join together to form a cluster of natural matter. Clusters of different shapes, arrangements and points form the natural world and the reality of the universe.
***Major exponent*:** Democritus (460–370 BC); see The Philosophy of Happiness

Conceptualism: the conceptualist philosopher views the metaphysical notion of universal absolutes from a perspective that refutes the presence of certain phenomena beyond the mind's perception of them. Hence, abstract ideas exist but only in people's thoughts.
***Major exponents*:** Gottfried Wilhelm Leibniz (1646–1716), David Hume (1711–76)

Consequentialism: an ethical paradigm centred on the notion that the moral value of an action is contingent on the action's consequence or result. A morally right or correct action in a given situation is one that produces a good outcome, and a morally wrong action is one that produces or has implicitly bad consequences.
***Major exponents*:** Epicurus (341–270 BC), Jeremy Bentham (1748–1832), John Stuart Mill (1806–73)

Deconstruction: a conceptual methodology for analyzing texts pioneered in the 1960s. Deconstruction aims to unravel the inner mechanics of how meaning in language is transferred and received in different cultural forms.
Major exponents: Paul de Man (1919–83), Jacques Derrida (1930–2004); see The Philosophy of Language

Deism: a belief system centred around the existence of a God/creator who is omnipresent, omnipotent and omnibenevolent.
Major exponents: too numerous to list such was the prevailing influence of theology on western scholastic philosophy; see The Philosophy of Religion

Deontology: the philosophical terminology that analyzes and evaluates the 'rightness' or 'wrongness' of an action as and of itself, regardless of the historical or probable consequences.
Major exponents: Immanuel Kant (1724–1804) and virtually everything that has occurred in the development of western philosophy in the last two centuries; see The Philosophy of Ethics and Morality

Determinism: the philosophical theory that all events, including moral choices, are determined entirely by previously existing causes.

***Major exponents*:** Zeno of Citium (332–262 BC), the founder of the Stoic school of Ancient Greek philosophy and his followers

Emotivism: a modern concept often used in psychoanalysis which posits that value judgements in relation to actions, especially ethical judgements, are born of emotional responses and are therefore subjective and unrepresentative of facts.
***Major exponents*:** Charles Stevenson (1908–79), A.J. Ayer (1910–89)

Empiricism: the theory that all knowledge is based on experience derived from the senses. Empiricism was motivated by the upsurge of experimental science and developed in the seventeenth and eighteenth centuries.
***Major exponents*:** John Locke (1632–1704), George Berkeley (1685–1753), David Hume (1711–76)

Epistemology: the study of the nature and possibility of knowledge, and how this translates into justified belief and relates intrinsically to concepts including truth, faith/belief and validation.
***Major exponent*:** René Descartes (1596–1650)

Existentialism: a twentieth-century philosophical theory or method of analysis that highlights the existence of the individual person as a free and responsible agent shaping their own development through acts of the will.
***Major exponents*:** Søren Kierkegaard (1813–55), arguably Friedrich Wilhelm Nietzsche (1844–1900), Jean-Paul Sartre (1905–80), Albert Camus (1913–60); see The Philosophy of Love

Idealism: certain systems of philosophical thought in which the objects of knowledge are held to be in some way dependent on the activity of mind.
***Major exponents*:** Immanuel Kant (1724–1804), Arthur Schopenhauer (1788–1860), arguably Friedrich Wilhelm Nietzsche (1844–1900)

Logical positivism: a philosophical movement developed by the Vienna Circle of intellectuals in the 1920s that promoted the view that scientific knowledge is the only kind of factual knowledge, and that all traditional metaphysical doctrines are to be rejected as meaningless.
***Major exponents*:** Ludwig Wittgenstein (1889–1951), Karl Popper (1902–94), A.J. Ayer (1910–89); see The Philosophy of Science

Materialism: the theory or belief that nothing exists except matter and its movements and modifications.
***Major exponents*:** Thomas Hobbes (1588–1679), Karl Marx (1818–1883), Gilles Deleuze (1925–95)

Metaphilosophy: an investigation into the nature of philosophy.
***Major exponent*:** Ludwig Wittgenstein (1889–1951)

Metaphysics: the branch of philosophy that studies the essence of something. The word derives from the Greek meaning 'beyond nature'. Typical areas of metaphysical enquiry include questions of being, becoming, existence, and reality.
***Major exponents*:** Aristotle defined metaphysics as 'first causes and the principles of things', and in this sense all philosophers from Socrates onwards, to one extent or another, have been exponents of metaphysical inquiry.

Monism: the metaphysical and theological view that all is one, that there are no fundamental divisions and that a unified set of laws underpins all of nature.
***Major exponents*:** (Ancient): Heraclitus of Ephesus (535–475 BC), Parmenides of Elea (dates uncertain); (Modern): Gottfried Wilhelm Leibniz (1646–1716), Georg Wilhelm Hegel (1770–1831), Arthur Schopenhauer (1788–1860)

Naturalism: the belief that nothing exists beyond the natural world and in denial of supernatural or spiritual explanations. It focuses on explanations that derive from observations of the laws of nature.
***Major exponents*:** Paul Kurtz (1925–2012), Roy Wood Sellars (1880–1973)

Nominalism: a philosophical view in metaphysics that denies the existence of universal and abstract objects but affirms the existence of general or abstract terms.
***Major exponents*:** William of Ockham (1285–1347), Thomas Hobbes (1588–1679)

Ontology: the area of metaphysics (see Nominalism) that examines the nature of being, first principles and unearthing the essence of things that exist.
***Major exponents*:** Bernard Bolzano (1781–1848), Franz Brentano (1838–1917), Gottlob Frege (1848–1925)

Panentheism/Pantheism: the belief that the divine pervades and interpenetrates every part of the universe and also extends beyond time and space. God is identified with the universe or the universe is a manifestation of God, making God and nature one.
***Major exponent*:** Baruch Spinoza (1632–1677)

Perspectivism: the philosophical position that our access to the world through perception, experience and reason is possible only through one's own perspective and interpretation. Therefore there are many possible conceptual schemes, or perspectives in which judgement of truth or value can be made.
***Major exponent*:** Friedrich Wilhelm Nietzsche (1844–1900)

Phenomenalism: the view that physical objects cannot justifiably be said to exist in themselves, but only as perceptual phenomena or sensory data situated in time and in space.
***Major exponent*:** John Stuart Mill (1806–73)

Postmodernism: a loose movement in the late 20th century encompassing art, literature, architecture and philosophy. A largely self-conscious approach that mixes different genres and forms. In philosophy, postmodernism is related to post-structuralism, addressing areas such as psychoanalysis, gender-studies, literature/discourse analysis and the history of ideas.
***Major exponents*:** Roland Barthes (1915–80), Michel Foucault (1926–84), Jacques Derrida (1930–2004)

Rationalism: reason rather than experience is the basis of conviction in knowledge, and rationalism asserts the epis-

temological view that regards reason as the chief source and test of knowledge.
***Major exponents*:** Pythagoras (570–495 BC), Plato (427–347 BC), Aristotle (384–322 BC), René Descartes (1596–1650), among countless others.

Realism: it accords to things that are known or perceived, an existence or nature that is independent of whether anyone is thinking about or perceiving them, and therefore ontologically independent of someone's conceptual scheme.
***Major exponents*:** David Hume (1711–76), Bertrand Russell (1872–1970), G.E. Moore (1873–1958)

Relativism: the doctrine that there are no absolute truths, i.e., that truth is always relative to some particular frame of reference, such as a language, culture or historical context, and so are not absolute.
***Major exponent*:** Paul Feyerabend (1924–94)

Solipsism: an extreme form of scepticism that denies the possibility of any knowledge other than one's own existence.
***Major exponents*:** René Descartes (1596–1650), George Berkeley (1685–1753)

Structuralism: a twentieth-century methodological theory in the humanities and social sciences that implies elements of human culture must be understood by way of their relationship to a broader, overarching system or structure. Structuralism aims to uncover the structures that underlie all the things that humans do, think, perceive and feel.
***Major exponents*:** Ferdinand de Saussure (1857–1913), Roman Jacobson (1896–1982), Claude Levi-Strauss (1908–2009)

Subjectivism: knowledge is simply subjective, without external or objective truth. In ethics, subjectivism is the meta-ethical belief that ethical propositions can be reduced to factual statements about the attitudes and/or conventions of individual people, or that any ethical sentence implies an attitude held by someone.
***Major exponents*:** René Descartes (1596–1650), Søren Kierkegaard (1813–55)

Teleology: the principle of final causality, which states explanations of phenomena by reference to some purpose, end, goal or function.
***Major exponent*:** Aristotle (384–322 BC)

Utilitarianism: a nineteenth-century philosophical position that determines the 'rightness' of an action according to its 'utility', and the extent to which it benefits the largest number of people.
***Major exponents*:** Jeremy Bentham (1748–1832), John Stuart Mill (1806–73)

SELECTED BIBLIOGRAPHY

Ayer, A.J., *The Central Questions of Philosophy* (Holt, London, 1974)

Blackburn, Simon (ed.), *Oxford Dictionary of Philosophy* (Oxford University Press, Oxford, 2008)

Blackburn, Simon, *Think: A Compelling Introduction to Philosophy* (Oxford University Press, Oxford, 1999)

Cahn, Stephen M., *Exploring Philosophy: An Introductory Anthology* (Oxford University Press, Oxford, 2008)

Craig, Edward, *Philosophy: A Very Short Introduction* (Oxford University Press, Oxford, 2002)

Critchley, Simon, *The Book of Dead Philosophers* (Granta, London, 2009)

Cudworth, Ralph, *The True Intellectual System of the Universe, Vol. I.* (New York: Gould & Newman, 1837, p. 267; first published 1678)

Darwin, Charles and Barlow, Nora (ed.), *The Autobiography of Charles Darwin 1809–1882.* With the original omissions restored. Edited and with appendix and notes by his granddaughter Nora Barlow. (Collins, London, 1958)

Foucault, Michel, *Discipline and Punish: The Birth of a Prison* (Penguin, London, 1991)

Foucault, Michel, *The History of Sexuality: The Will to Knowledge* (Penguin, London, 1998)

Gaarder, Jostein, *Sophie's World* (Weidenfeld & Nicolson, London, 1991)

Garner, Richard T. and Rosen, Bernard, *Moral Philosophy: A Systematic Introduction to Normative Ethics and Meta-ethics* (Macmillan, New York, 1967)

Grayling, A.C., *The Meaning of Things* (Weidenfeld & Nicholson, London, 2001)

Kagan, Shelly, *The Limits of Morality* (Clarendon Press, Oxford, 1989, p. 17n)

Kaufman, Walter, *Existentialism from Dostoyevsky to Sartre* (New American Library, New York, 1975)

Kohl, Herbert, *The Age of Complexity* (Mentor Books Ltd, New York, 1965)

Levene, Lesley, *I Think, Therefore I Am* (Michael O'Mara Books Ltd, London, 2010)

Mautner, Thomas (ed.), *Penguin Dictionary of Philosophy* (Penguin Books, London, 1997)

Monk, Ray and Raphael, Frederic, *The Great Philosophers* (Weidenfeld & Nicholson, London, 2000)

Nagel, Thomas, *What Does It All Mean?* (Oxford University Press, Oxford, 2004)

Paley, William, *Natural Theology: or, Evidences of the Existence and Attributes of the Deity* 12th ed., (J. Faulder, London, 1809)

Pirie, Madsen, *101 Great Philosophers: Makers of Modern Thought* (Bloomsbury, London, 2009)

Rabinow, Paul (ed.), *The Foulcault Reader: An Introduction to Foulcault's Thought* (Penguin, London, 1991)

Ross, W. D., *The Right and the Good*, (Oxford University Press, Oxford, 1930; reprinted with an introduction by Philip Stratton-Lake, 2002)

Rowe, William L., *The Problem of Evil and Some Varieties of Atheism*. Reprinted in Howard-Snyder, Daniel (ed.), *The Evidential Argument from Evil* (Indiana University Press, Bloomington, IN, 1996)

Russell, Bertrand, *History of Western Philosophy* (Allen & Unwin Ltd, London, 1961)

Sartre, Jean-Paul, *Being and Nothingness* (Routledge, London, 1943)

Sartre, Jean-Paul, *Existentialism and Humanism* (Methuen, London, 2007)

Singer, Peter, *The Life You Can Save* (Random House, New York and London, 2010)

Suits, Bernard, *The Grasshopper: Games, Life and Utopia* (Broadview Press, London, 2005)

Urmson, J.O. and Ree, Jonathan, *The Concise Encyclopaedia of Western Philosophy & Philosophers* (Routledge, New York and London, 1989)

Wainwright, W.J., *The Oxford Handbook of Philosophy of Religion* (Oxford Handbooks Online, 2004)

Warburton, Nigel, *Philosophy: The Basics* (Routledge, London, 2012)

Yandell, K.E., *Philosophy of Religion – A Contemporary Introduction* (Routledge, London, 2002)

ACKNOWLEDGEMENTS

I would like to thank the following people for their help, support and advice in writing and compiling this book: Louise Dixon, my commissioning editor at Michael O'Mara Books for suggesting the project to me. I really appreciate your continuing faith and support. Emily Thomas, my new editor, for her diligence, almost limitless patience and hard work, plus the rest of the design, sales and production team at MOM. The library and information services staff at the University of Sussex for the use of their excellent facilities and putting up with me nodding off at my laptop from time to time for a power nap. Mr Steve Trees, Edward 'Butch' Dykes and the rest of the 'daytime philosophers' for their generosity, support, advice and encouragement throughout the process. And, finally, my family, friends and my wife Joanna and daughter Polly for their love and encouragement, and for putting up with my idiosyncratic timekeeping and spouting of esoteric theories. My sincerest thanks to you all.

INDEX